MARKETING RESEARCH

QUALITATIVE METHODS FOR THE MARKETING PROFESSIONAL

Daniel T. Seymour

PROBUS PUBLISHING COMPANY

Chicago, Illinois

This publication is designed to provide accurate and authoritative information in regard to the subject matter covered. It is sold with the understanding that the publisher is not engaged in rendering legal, accounting or other professional service. If legal advice or other expert assistance is required, the services of a competent professional person should be sought.

FROM A DECLARATION OF PRINCIPLES JOINTLY ADOPTED BY A COMMITTEE OF THE AMERICAN BAR ASSOCIATION AND A COMMITTEE OF PUBLISHERS.

Library of Congress Cataloging in Publication Data Available

ISBN 0-917253-89-2

Printed in the United States of America

1 2 3 4 5 6 7 8 9 0

DEDICATION

To Ray and Kate

PREFACE

There are no two ways about it: qualitative research is messy. Asking people how they feel about something often leads to "streams of consciousness." Their replies can be lengthy and filled with contradictions. They can describe in elaborate detail the true motivations behind an action, or they can recount a complex maze of irrelevant wanderings. In the same way, recording various behaviors can leave the observer frustrated— "What does it all mean?" Also, the samples are small, not projectable and hence not representative of the total population. The resulting information provides intuition and empathy but does not provide a decision maker the comfort of increased certainty.

And yet the fact is that qualitative research is being used by brand managers, marketing and advertising researchers, professors and students, and decision makers at all levels in all kinds of organizations. Unfortunately, there continues to be a great tendency in the qualitative area to be nonchalant concerning the specifics of the techniques. Any individual with a B.A. in Psychology feels competent to set up shop as a market research consultant. Today, more often than not, any research design is initiated with the words, "Let's do some groups." And in carrying out the design using qualitative research techniques, anything goes. Qualitative methods are no less rigorous than quantitative, but because the data are messy we have a tendency to be less exacting. Such laxness only serves to lessen the value of information and, in the long run, results in the disuse of a set of techniques that should be of great value to the research community.

What needs to be said, then, is quite simple: "We've got a good thing here. But if we don't watch it, if we don't pay attention to the grimy details, if we continue to misapply techniques, and if we continue in our casual ways, qualitative techniques in consumer research will be put back on the shelf." The reason for such a demise would not be any inherent difficulties with the techniques, but rather the lack of commitment in incorporating the necessary rigor into the research process.

Marketing Research: Qualitative Methods for the Marketing Professional is intended for those individuals who are doing and using decision-oriented research. As we will see, this book stresses a relationship between problem identification, technique choice, information generation, and increased understanding. The choice of a particular research technique, whether qualitative or quantitative, is driven by the nature of the problem. The information that results, in turn, needs to be matched to the kind of understanding that is required. This book is for the marketing and advertising professionals who are continually faced with the difficulty of generating information about consumers. Such professionals are faced with a series of tradeoffs—cost versus timeliness, complexity versus simplicity, technique strengths versus technique weaknesses. Whether it is a brand manager, an advertising researcher or copywriter, a member of a new product development team, a vice president of marketing, or a consumer researcher, the bottom line is still the same—increased understanding.

The qualitative techniques discussed in this book have quite varied histories. Some amount of time is taken, therefore, in giving the reader a glimpse at these electic backgrounds. The real substance or heart of the book, however, is contained in the many sections which describe the techniques and enumerate in detail the strengths and weaknesses of each. The extensive use of previous research and current management examples reinforces the fact that this book is for the practitioner. As such, research rhetoric is kept to a minimum, and advice kept to practical applications. The marketing professional is in need of just such practical, down-home wisdom when it comes to the use of qualitative research techniques. Unfortunately, much of what is being used today is handed down; much of what is being said is folklore. Those articles, monographs, and books that discuss the subject are often sophomoric, carrying such titles as "What to Wear to Your Next Focus Group."

Chapter One, *Setting the Stage,* is an overview of a number of themes that are common to all chapters in the book. After defining "qualitativeness," attention is turned toward the nature of the qualitative/quantitative dichotomy. A review of this dichotomy is designed to show that the different research approaches can be seen in something other than a competitive structure. This non-competitiveness theme is followed by a problem-orientation theme. The objective in this section is to caution against the tendency to base research designs on the researcher's "favorite techniques." The final theme stresses a multi-level view of the consumer. Information and meaning about consumers' behaviors, attitudes, and motivations occur on different levels. The various techniques that are available to a consumer researcher have vastly different capabilities at differing levels of meaning.

Chapter Two, *Integrating Research Techniques,* presents a comparative analysis of qualitative and quantitative research approaches. The capabilities and limitations of both perspectives are described. The necessary insights into the two research approaches are developed in order to aid the marketing professional in the design and use of research that capitalizes on the strengths of the various qualitative and quantitative techniques.

The technique chapters, Three through Seven, are arranged in a specific order—from the most direct, observable information to the most indirect, hidden information. This ordering represents different "levels of meaning" beginning with a technique for describing consumers' buying behavior and ending with a method to explore consumers' motivations. The techniques of Chapter Three are known as *Observation Methods* because the researcher "observes" the things that are happening; no questions are asked, no surveys completed. The major benefit of such observation is that the resulting behaviors occur naturally, a stream of human performances unaltered by a researcher's intrusive questioning. The group of qualitative techniques known as unobtrusive measures, participant observation and protocol analysis all provide such qualitative, descriptive data.

The techniques of Chapter Four, *Group Interviewing,* do more than just describe behaviors—they attempt to enumerate the reasonings, the rationalizations which drive observable acts. Such interviewing in marketing and advertising had its origins in the area of group psychological therapy, where the concept is based on the assumption that individuals who share a problem or concern will be more willing to discuss it within the security provided by others sharing the same problem. When applied to business situations, however, group interviewing techniques have proven useful in a different manner. They are excellent tools for idea generation, detailing consumption systems (how people use things), and instigating discussions concerning commonly known topics among the group members (such as political candidates, a new brokerage service product for a bank, or a series of advertisements for a hotel chain). It should be noted, however, that while these techniques do generate attitudes, opinions and beliefs, they are only on the surface, and do not represent the more complex motivational structure of human behavior.

Depth Interviewing is the topic of Chapter Five. The obvious difference between group interviewing and depth interviewing is that the latter technique is one-on-one: participants are limited to the researcher and the subject. The emphasis shifts to individual feelings. As such, the depth interview has been the principal diagnostic and therapeutic tool of modern psychiatry. It has the ability to reveal complex sentiments which underlie an expressed opinion. Not just the surface opinions which connote an "appropriate" public response, but the more detailed, hidden aspects of the inner self. This level of meaning is such that an interviewer must have the time and privacy to probe beyond immediate surface-type responses. With depth interviewing the researcher can employ an entire set of tactics that have proven to be very successful at penetrating the public self which individuals show the world.

Chapter Six is entitled *Projective Methods*. The techniques discussed in this chapter are used to explore the most basic level of meaning characterized by impulses, prejudices, predispositions, drives and desires. In marketing and advertising research we know that by using group-interviewing and depth-interviewing methods we can generate the basic set of attitudes and opinions which underly consumer behavior. Such techniques, however, are usually not suitable for probing into the psycholgical or sociological determinants of those "voiced" attitudes. The deeper we go with levels of meaning the more repressed the concepts are. For instance, drives often exist below a level of awareness such that the individual is not consciously aware of them—or cannot articulate them. Motivational methods, therefore, represent the most refined techniques for understanding the basic drives and desires which are ultimately manifested in consumers' behaviors.

The final chapter, *Managing Qualitative Research*, is concerned with the effective management of qualitative information within the overall research process. The extent of the market research function in organizations is directly related to the need for information. That is, as the need for market information has grown, the size and role of research has changed. For example, while market research had traditionally been concerned with the tactical decisions of brand and product managers, under the broadened umbrella of strategic planning the horizons of marketing research have been broadened to encompass policy issues and decisions involved with allocations of corporate resources. Not only has the role of research become more planning-oriented, providing input at a higher level in an organization, it has also become more widely applied. It is apparent, then, that as the use of market research information increases within an organization, more attention should be paid to managing the information flow. Since the expanded role of marketing research in organizations has resulted in more direct involvement of many different users, it is important to see what effect qualitative data has on this interaction. And it follows that the ability of the user and supplier to understand their respective views will impact the value of information which is generated.

Finally, it needs to be re-emphasized that the theme to this book is serviceability—ideas and techniques that are based on sound logic and are practical tools in our attempt to understand human behavior in the consumption process. Such a grand notion does have a historical precedent: Oliver Cromwell addressed his troops as they were about to cross a river to attack the enemy. He concluded with the famous exhortation: "Put your trust in God, but mind you keep your powder dry."

The time is right for a healthy dose of Cromwellian usefulness.

Daniel T. Seymour

CONTENTS

CHAPTER ONE

SETTING THE STAGE

Three times a month, Ronna Jernigan commands the attention of the nation's leading food manufacturers. The diminutive 28-year-old Jernigan has the General Foods, Ralston Purinas and General Mills of the world snapping to as she unloads their products onto the checkout counter. Each time she gives the checkout clerk a numbered red card that is keyed into the supermarket's scanner. If she chooses Post Toasties over Cheerios, General Foods may be happy, but General Mills may scratch its head. General Mills may be puzzled because it will know that Jernigan, or her husband, Scott, or one of their daughters, Leanne, or Sara, has seen a Cheerios commercial—or 10 such commercials—since last she shopped.

In the Jernigan living room in the nearby suburb of SpringdayHills, a large brown box monitors the Jernigans' television viewing habits. Each evening, the day's viewing record is sent through telephone lines to an ERIM computer to record whether the Jernigans watched the Jell-O ad on ABC or the Cheerios ad on CBS. General Mills is one of a growing list of national advertisers who pay princely sums to Electronic Research Insights into Marketing (ERIM), a division of Northbrook, Illinois-based Nielsen Marketing Research, to track the Jernigan purchases and television viewing habits.[1]

ERIM is just one of the latest gadgets being used in consumer research to aid marketing decision-makers. Other technological wizardry includes automated interviewing terminals, scanners, eye tracking cameras, voice pitch analysis, and videotex.

These measurement devices can be useful in establishing associations between various stimuli (advertisements) and responses (purchase behaviors). They are especially good at counting things—how many, how often, in what order. And as such, the resulting data can be gathered in large quantities and subjected to various statistical tests and controlled experiments. For instance, in our ERIM example the director of marketing research for General Mills comments that: "We can split the people in Springfield and Sioux Falls into two matched groups and watch for four weeks to see what happens when we give 30 ads to one and 50 to the other. On the average, have we sold more products in one than the other?"

3

The understanding that comes from quantitative data is important and useful to marketing professionals. But it is a limited kind of understanding. It does not provide insights into attitudes, motivations, contexts, or impressions. It gives the dimensions of a sailboat but not the feeling of the wind in the sails. It measures the percentage of teenagers who said that they would recommend a new movie to a friend but not how a teenager identified with the main character; it registers figures but not feelings. The reader may have been introduced to qualitative research by one of many different labels—motivational research, depth interviewing, focus groups, unobtrusive measures or, perhaps, "touchy feely." Such terms can describe a particular technique, a method of inquiry or a particular researcher's bias. It is much more appropriate, however, to view qualitative research as one of the general ways in which *data can be collected:*

> Qualitative data consist of detailed descriptions of situations, events, people, interactions, and observed behaviors; direct quotations from people about their experiences, attitudes, beliefs, and thoughts; and excerpts or entire passages from documents, correspondence, records, and case histories.[2]

Qualitative research, therefore, should be thought of as an array of methods and approaches which attempt to generate information without predetermined categories; concern is with the essence and meaning of communication in its natural form. From such a perspective, qualitative methods are quite similar to the interpretive procedures we make as we go about our everyday lives. The data we collect and act upon in everyday life are impressionistic and reactive:

> When crossing the street, for example, the sight of a ten-ton truck bearing down on us leads to an immediate and presumably prudent action. We do not stop to first ask how fast the truck is traveling, from where did it come, how often does this occur, or what is the driver's intention. We move.[3]

The truck, simply, is a symbol and our reaction is based upon an impression of that symbol—danger! Qualitative research attempts to identify such symbols, and as a way of assessing their meaning, record and interpret the pattern of responses these symbols elicit. The data describe peoples' experiences in their own terms.

The collection of qualitative data, therefore, stands in stark contrast to quantitative data collection procedures which impose a predetermined framework upon respondents. The researcher develops a series of categories and respondents are asked to fit their attitudes, opinions and behaviors into the appropriate slots. Our pedestrian could be asked the following questions:

1. Please indicate how fast the truck was traveling in miles per hour:

0-15 mph	16-25 mph	26-35 mph	36-45 mph	46-55 mph	56 + mph

2. Mark the direction from which the truck was traveling:

East	West	North	South

3. How ofen do you find yourself in dangerous confrontations with trucks?

Always	Usually	Sometimes	Never

The benefits from collecting data in such slots and pigeonholes are substantial. We can now survey a representative sample of pedestrians and add up our categories. We can calculate such quantitative niceties as means, modes and medians. We can even derive the proportion of trucks which travel at 56 mph *and* are southward bound.

On the other hand, a qualitative approach would result in data which describe what peoples' experiences mean *in their own terms,* as opposed to a researcher's. A simple question such as "Describe for me the events surrounding your confrontation with the truck?" may well elicit a more meaningful description of the incident we are studying. The resulting data would reflect what was important to the respondent, a description of the event as they saw it. By adopting a qualitative data gathering approach, the researcher has made a commitment to get close to people and situations in a process of discovery.

Before plunging into the mechanics of qualitative research, there are a number of general topics that act as themes for this book. They are common threads that are stated and restated in each chapter. The importance of these themes cannot be overemphasized. So often in research, and other areas, we want to get on with the business at hand. Little, if any, time is spent in attempting to gain a solid foundation of understanding. Three themes are as important to marketing and advertising professionals as any of the details of the various techniques and represent the much-needed foundation on which the successful use of qualitative techniques depend:

Figures and Feelings. There has been an increasing tendency for researchers to adopt one position and reject the other. A "figures" person identifies with the positive advantages from generating a data base and analyzing the numbers. A "feelings" person is enamored with the benefits derived from having a chance to elicit emotions. Each person, however, often fails to see clearly the disadvantages of their own methods and the advantages of the rejected methods. The Electronic Research Insights into Marketing (ERIM) method and data provides an illustration. Does it tell the full story? No. Is it useful information? Absolutely. The fact is that figures and feelings are quite compatible and, oftentimes, are even complementary.

Problem Oriented. One of the most unfortunate by-products of the qualitative/quantitative dichotimization is a certain ritualization of methods. It is not that uncommon for a researcher to become overly dependent on a technique or group of techniques. Much like the saying "An accident looking for a place to happen," the result of this myopia is "A solution method looking for a problem." Is the ERIM approach the right way to go? It depends. The answer to the question is dependent upon the management problem. And that is where all research should begin.

Levels of Meaning. Psychologists have spent a great deal of time researching "personality" and "meaning." In general, each person exists at different levels—the outermost level is that which is most readily apparent to others. This outer-surface is exposed to the public and is measured in a straightforward fashion (e.g. demographic questions). The most repressed level is the private self that is not exposed to public view and becomes manifest only through indirect means (e.g. psychoanalytic procedures). The ERIM procedure is able to generate stacks of data on a large number of families' purchase behaviors because it is only attempting to gather surface-level information. Such electronic research, however, is incapable of tapping closely-held motivations.

CHOOSING BETWEEN FIGURES AND FEELINGS

There is no reason to expect marketing to be exempt from the same division that has been evident in such other disciplines as sociology and psychology. There are sociologists who swear by participant observation and psychologists who swear by experimentation. The two camps have been known to disagree with a good deal of fervor. And marketers have the same sense of impassioned territorialism. Some of the more articulate pro-qualitative comments include:

"Nowhere is it written in stone that the acquisition of knowledge must be statistically projectable to constitute knowledge."[4]

"Quantitative research insofar as it purports to talk about consumer behavior, transforms real people into abstract categories so that it can put numbers along each side of the categories."[5]

"I would like to state that using purely descriptive techniques when we are basically interested in interpretation and understanding of behavior and the application of this knowledge is not only erroneous but unscientific and dangerously misleading."[6]

"Today the social scientists are enamored of numbers and counting. Rarely do they stop and ask, 'What lies behind the numbers?'"[7]

Since the "feelings" people have had their turn, it is only fair that the "figures" people be allowed to respond to these rather pointed criticisms:

" . . . the greatest danger in qualitative research is that it purports to contain the entire answer—the findings are usually presented in such a way that the user is lulled into believing that the statements concerned really do apply to the majority."[8]

"The very complexity of social events requires a language of quantity. For, wherever it is possible to 'codify' there is a better opportunity to teach as well as to learn."[9]

" . . . they should be able to come up with quantitative findings. As well as being more useful, this is a requisite of the scientific approach. It is also one more reason why definitive reactions to stimuli must be studied rather than opinions, attitudes, and preferences, which as such cannot be reduced to weights or measures."[10]

As can be seen, both sides are articulate in their views and very determined. But while it is reasonable to assume that the goal of truth is similar whether you are a "feelings" person or a "figures" person, the perception is, apparently, that the approach to truth realization is vastly different. Such parochialism reinforces a unidimensional view of the consumer. A view that is limiting and simplisitic. The fact remains that these biased perceptions are both unfortunate and generally misleading:

Philosophically it is a near meaningless dichotomy which if sustained too long has a baleful effect on the disputants. It induces myopia and mental rigidity, and its naive foundations quickly need moralistic evaluations that have no place in applied science.[11]

Rather than dwelling on the specific differences inherent in the qualitative/quantitative dichotomy, it is certainly more beneficial to emphasize the complementary traits of each approach. The overall reward from this more "accepting" view is the possibility of using multiple approaches in a research design. The astute researcher can oscillate between the two approaches, utilizing the strengths of each to increase the value of information.

During the last two decades many investigators have tried to determine how blood donors differ from nondonors. Unfortunately, the application of findings have not been very successful. Only eight to nine percent of the eligible donors remain active. In a 1981 study, Burnett attempted to delineate new demographic and behavioral characteristics of blood donors and nondonors. Initially, seven separate focus groups of donors and nondonors were conducted. The results of the focus interviews confirmed several of the variables which had been identified by previous investigators. In addition, three new constructs were identified: "blood type," "general health salience," and "conservatism/liberalism." The resulting variable list was used in a mail survey which was distributed to a random sample of donors and nondonors. The data generated from the survey was then submitted to a stepwise multiple discriminant program. An analysis of the coefficients suggested that donors could be described and distinguished from nondonors on the basis of a number of the demographic, personality and attitude variables.

The qualitative research, in this case, was used to confirm the existence of some variables that had been described in previous studies. As such, it provided a subjective replication of quantitatively derived variables. The focus group interviews also resulted in several new variables and acted in a hypothesis generation manner. Finally, quantitative survey data were analyzed using a multivariate statistical technique.

BECOMING PROBLEM ORIENTED

The proliferation of marketing research techniques is a mixed blessing. While the additional tools increase the level of sophistication available to consumer researchers, it has also proceeded to overwhelm most researchers. To be able to apply routinely a large number of techniques to different management problems, while also "gearing up" on the latest technique, is a somewhat arduous task. Unfortunately, the scenario usually goes as follows: one begins to specialize in a class of techniques due to training, interest, competency or workload; one loses contact with the procedures and applications of other techniques; and finally, one rationalizes the wisdom of his or her chosen techniques to any and all who will listen. While the excuses are numerous and the rationalizations understandable, the bottom line is that there is a serious myopia in the design of methodology for its own sake. It is, simply, "Not unlike the running of railroads for the sake of steam, whistles, track, and locomotives, rather than for moving freight and passengers."[13]

Technical expertise and specialization is desirable but the enchantment with a specific method is counterproductive. The techniques used to collect and analyze marketing information should be decided by the needs of the research itself. That is, the operational use of the findings must dictate how those findings are to be generated and in what form.

Package designers say even if you can't afford a big advertising budget, you've got a fighting chance if your product displays a compelling image from the shelf. So it would make sense to rush right out and hire a package designer and let him work some magic for your product. "Wrong," says Tom Keyser, packaging supervisor with the household and houseware products division of 3M Company. "The first thing you do is figure out what your marketing problems are." Why? "Because it will be very important for you to select a design group that can solve your kind of problem. You'll want to look for a package design company that has demonstrated a wide range of problem-solving abilities, not one that takes 'Plan B' off the shelf and plugs it into your problem.[14]

Package design is only one of the many and extremely varied kinds of problems that may need to be analyzed by marketing professionals. Each class of problems poses its own unique set of questions, and each demands its own unique set of research methods to supply the necessary answers.

UNDERSTANDING LEVELS OF MEANING

The final, and most important, theme provides the structure for the organization of this book. The idea of "levels of meaning" is derived from the commonly held notion that personality exists on several different levels. Kurt Lewin, for example, saw the individual as a series of concentric circles—the smallest circle, consists of the most personal and intimate personality components. This is a "repressed" level, potentially embarrassing if it was revealed. A second circle involves more public motives, attitudes and emotions but those that the individual still does not readily divulge. The most remote circle is that which is most psychologically distant from the individual and, as such, is the most easily verbalized.

For our purposes, "levels of meaning" can be viewed as a vertical continuum from conscious activities to unconscious activities (see the table on page 11).[15] The different Meaning levels can be accessed via different Methods. And it follows that each Method generates a different kind of Output.

The top level of Meaning, *Descriptive*, is concerned with the conscious description of behaviors. Such behaviors are psychologically the most distant from the individual because they represent publicly-witnessed actions. The researcher can use any number of Methods to generate information at this level. The public Output to this level are immediate, spontaneous responses that are either easily observed or to which numbers can be readily assigned. The techniques discussed in Chapter Three are known as "Observational Methods" because the researcher "observes" the things that are happening; no questions are asked, no surveys completed. The resulting behaviors occur naturally, a stream of human performances unaltered by a researcher's intrusive questioning.

Meaning	Method	Output	
Descriptive	Observation Survey	Immediate spon- taneous responses	
Conscious Spontaneous responses	Experiments Panel	Observable acts	*Public*
Outer-Self	Group Interview Open-ended	Justifications Rationalizations	
Reasoned			
Inner-Self	Depth Interview	Elaborations Introspections	
Concealed			
Motive	Motivational	Repressions Symbols	
Uncon- scious Predisposed			*Private*

Moving down the continuum we pass through a level of Meaning that exhibits *Outer Self* characteristics. The techniques discussed in Chapter Four, "Group Interviewing," do more than just describe behaviors, they attempt to enumerate the reasonings, the rationalizations, that explain observable acts. Such interviewing in marketing and advertising had its origins in the area of group psychological therapy where the concept is based on the assumption that individuals who share a problem or concern will be more willing to discuss it within the security of others sharing the same problem. When applied to business-related situations, however, group interviewing techniques have proven useful in a different manner. They are excellent tools for idea generation, detailing consumption systems (how people use things), and for instigating discussions concerning commonly known topics among the group members (e.g. political candidates, a new brokerage service product for a bank, or a series of advertisements). It can be noted from the table, however, that while these Methods do generate attitude, opinion and belief Output, they are surface in nature and do not represent the more complex motivational structure of human behavior.

The *Inner Self* information is a level of Meaning that penetrates the shell of the individual. As such it relates to more closely-held beliefs. "Depth Interviewing," Chapter Five, details techniques that are superior at gathering information of this sort. The obvious difference between group interviewing and depth interviewing is that the latter technique is one-on-one; participants are limited to the researcher and the subject. The emphasis shifts to the individual. As such, the depth interview has been the principal diagnostic and therapeutic tool of modern psychiatry. It has the ability to reveal more complex sentiments that underlie an expressed opinion; not just the Outer-Self opinions that connote an "appropriate" public response, but the more detailed introspections of the Inner-Self.

Finally, the *Motivation* level of the continuum deals with information that an individual may be unable or unwilling to express. A series of techniques contained in Chapter Six, "Motivational Methods," have proven to be extremely useful at discerning meaning at this unconscious level characterized by impulses, prejudices, predispositions, drives and desires. In marketing and advertising we know that by using group interviewing and depth interviewing methods we can generate the basic set of attitudes and opinions which underly consumer behavior. Such techniques, however, are usually not suitable for probing into the psycholgical or sociological determinants of those "voiced" attitudes. Drives often exist below a level of awareness such that the individual is not consciously aware of them—or cannot articulate them. Other techniques, therefore, must be used to generate and understand the meaning of basic drives and desires that are ultimately manifested in consumers' symbols and behaviors.

A fundamental aspect of marketing and advertising research, then, is to match the Method to the Meaning in order to generate the informational Output that is most appropriate for the consumer process under investigation.

Selling a World's Fair to North Americans isn't easy anymore. New Orleans found out the hard way—its $350 million fair went bankrupt in 1984 after failing to attract big crowds. That disaster helped persuade Chicago to cancel plans for a 1992 fair and created concern in Vancouver, the Western Canadian city that hosted the $1.1 billion exposition based on a transportation and communications theme. Expo 86 had to reach out to attract tourists. Only 12 million people live within a one-and-a-half-day drive of Vancouver, the area normally considered the prime market for such a fair.

The marketing staff undertook several research studies after British Columbia's premier, William Bennett, took a trip to California during the previous summer and discovered that few people in the state had even heard of the fair. Thousands of telephone interviews were conducted to generate a basic set of descriptive data on vacation habits. One result of this study was the knowledge that advance planning takes only four to 12 weeks for a typical North American family vacationing by car. This resulted in Expo 86 marketers deciding to hold off on high cost TV spending until the fall in order to concentrate their ads.

Also, a series of focus group sessions were conducted. One significant finding in this study proved very important to the ultimate success of Expo 86. It was discovered that the assurance of "hospitality" was critical to many peoples' vacation plans. Therefore, instead of spending funds on originally scheduled celebrity testimonial advertisements, a world-wide mailing of 1.3 million personal invitations were sent. The invitations, signed by Premier Bennett, were sent to addresses that were provided by local citizens—the letter invited them to visit both the fair and a British Columbia friend or relative named in the letter.[16]

The telephone data gathered by the Expo 86 marketers proved most appropriate for addressing a certain level of understanding. Media scheduling is an advertising problem that requires a basic descriptive knowledge of consumer buying habits. Such meaning exists at a very approachable level. In contrast, more complex and personally held explanations are found at another level of meaning. A major communications appeal was based on the "hospitality" explanation. A stratification of meaning existed for the activity—"going on vacation." This stratification is useful in that it is a viable means for organizing, evaluating, and discriminating between different research techniques and the kind of information they are capable of producing.

FINALITIES

The Paleontologist

An example from a discipline far removed from Marketing may be useful in summarizing the three themes discussed above. A paleontologist may go into the field to further his or her understanding of a particular type of fossil. At first, the researcher uses experience and knowledge to direct him to certain sedimentary rocks which have, in the past, yielded such specimens. Having found a potentially productive geographic area, lines are paced off and a thorough documentation of the site is undertaken; precise locality, remarks on kind and thickness of rocks, and other measures yield information on the history of the surroundings. The quarrying phase usually involves the use of an assortment of sledge hammers, wedges, chisels and pry bars. Such tools are not randomly applied but rather are chosen to pursue a line of endeavor. A crack or fracture may necessitate certain equipment to split the structure so that fresh surfaces may be exposed. As the pursuit continues, different tools are used for increasingly delicate work until the actual removal of a fossil from the rock is attempted. Here again, equipment such as various acids, dental picks, or vibro-tools are used to dislodge the object, followed by surface cleaning with acetone, alcohol, or other solutions with the aid of a stereoscopic microscope. And finally, the internal structure can be studied using serial grinding techniques or needle dissections.

The knowledge that the paleontologist gains is the result of a series of decisions which entail matching research problems with the kind of information derived from a set of techniques. The ten pound sledge hammer yields a certain level of understanding, while the needle dissection is somewhat better suited to another problem. The tools of the trade, in this case, are much more graphic, but the process of interrelating techniques, "levels of meaning", and research problems is similar to the task faced by the marketing professional in attempting to gain a better understanding of the consumer.

Managerial Insights

The marketing professional should pay particular attention to the following insights in the course of the design of consumer research studies:

Broaden Technique Use. The marketing professional should treat all techniques as potentially valuable for understanding the consumer. Thomas Carlyle, the Scottish essayist and historian, once noted "Man is a tool-using animal . . . Without tools he is nothing, with tools he is all."[17] It is indeed unfortunate that some consumer researchers ignore some tools that could be of great aid. Such self-limitation can be overcome if researchers can forsake the tendency to latch onto a few favorite techniques.

Become Problem-oriented. The ultimate objective of research is to generate information which is capable of reducing the risk in decision making. At the same time, the perception is that the capable consumer researcher should get on with solving the problem—seeking brilliant solutions. Researchers should spend more time in formulating, analyzing and organizing the problem and resist the urge to "get on with it." This is not the easiest thing in the world to do. All the focus is on seeking answers. If the questions, however, are improperly derived, the solutions are not going to be of much use.

Bring Problem And Technique Together. The kind of information generated in a study is dependent upon the technique employed; and the kind of technique employed is dependent upon the problem definition. Trying to give your car a tune-up in the family garage can be a laborious task, regardless of your inate mechanical ability. The auto mechanic can usually do a faster, more effective job because he has all the specialized tools to change the spark plugs, adjust the timing chain, and so on. While cars have become increasingly complex, they still do not approach the complexity of man—or Joe and Josephine Consumer. The techniques (tools) used to collect and analyze consumer information should be decided by the needs of the research problem.

ENDNOTES

[1]Gorman, John (1987), "Tracking the Consumer," *The Providence Journal* (March 15), p. F1.

[2]Patton, Michael (1980), *Qualitative Evaluation Methods* (Beverly Hills: Sage Publications, Inc.), p. 22.

[3]Van Maanen, J. (1979), "Reclaiming Qualitative Methods for Organizational Research: A Preface," *Administration Science Quarterly*, p. 521.

[4]Fleischman, Andrew M. (1982), "Qualitative Is Marketing Research Because It Aids Decision Makers, Helps Reduce Risk," *Marketing News* (January 22), p. 8.

[5]Cowl, John (1972), "Numbers Good—Feelings Better (or Climbing Out of the Anthill)," *Australian Journal of Marketing Research* (February), p. 12.

[6]Dichter, Ernest (1978), "Interpretative Versus Descriptive Research," in *Research in Marketing*, J. Sheth (ed.), (JAI Press: Greenwich) p. 56.

[7]Gardner, Burleigh (1978), *Marketing News* (May 5), p. 1.

[8]Nowick, Henry (1972), "Figures or Feelings," *Australian Journal of Marketing Research* (February), p. 9.

[9]Zeisel, Hans (1957), *Say It With Figures* (Harper and Brothers Publishers: New York), p. xv.

[10]Politz, Alfred (1957), "Science and Truth in Marketing Research," *Harvard Business Review* 35 (January-February), p. 119.

[11]Meadows, Arthur W. (1972), "Quantitative or Qualitative or—What?," *Australian Journal of Marketing Research* (February), p. 23.

[12]Burnett, John J. (1981), "Psychographic and Demographic Characteristics of Blood Donors," *Journal of Consumer Research* 8 (June), p. 62.

[13]Andrus, Roman and James Reinmuth (1979), "Avoid Research Myopia in Marketing Analysis," *Business Horizons* (June), p. 55.

[14]Kesler, Lori (1981), "Shopping Around for a Design," *Advertising Age* (December 28), ps-1.

[15]Adapted from: Lannon, Judie (1986), "New Techniques for Understanding Consumer Reactions to Advertising," *Journal of Advertising Research* 26 (August-September), p. RC-8.

[16]Bayless, Alan (1986), "Vancouver Tests a New Recipe for Promoting a World's Fair," *The Wall Street Journal* (February 5), p. 27.

[17]Carlyle, Thomas (1838), *Sir Walter Scott*.

CHAPTER TWO

INTEGRATING RESEARCH TECHNIQUES

The goal of this chapter is to crystalize the nature of the interrelationship and interdependence of both qualitative and quantitative methodologies and data. The contention is that the astute researcher alternates between the two approaches using the strengths of each. In fact, the methods are like two halves of an orange; properly conducted both can give an accurate though segmented accounting of the object under study. But complete understanding is best gained by a combination of the two. The position advocated is, really, quite simple—avoid being for or against quantification or qualification as if it were an either/or issue. The only sensible course to pursue is that of the proverbial "fence sitter."

> To some extent the battle lines correlate with a relative concern for "hardness" versus "depth and reality" of data. Quantitative data are often thought of as "hard," and qualitative as "real and deep"; thus if you prefer "hard" data you are for quantification and if you prefer "real, deep" data you are for qualitative participant observation. What to do if you prefer data that are real, deep and hard is not immediately apparent.[1]

By understanding the capabilities and limitations of the approaches, the fence sitter is in a unique position to exploit both methods and consequently to gain an overall understanding of the complexities of human behavior from data that are real, deep and hard.

Obviously, such an integrative approach to research can only increase the value of whatever qualitative research techniques are used. But the fact is that the qualitative/quantitative dichotomy is well entrenched in Marketing. We should not, however, feel unique in our biases. The *tete-a-tete* has a long-standing and expansive tradition. For example, Lord Kelvin proclaimed in 1891:

> When you can measure what you are speaking about, and express it in numbers, you know something about it; but when you cannot measure it, when you cannot express it in numbers, your knowledge is a meager and unsatisfactory kind: it may be the beginning of knowledge, but you have scarcely, in your thoughts, advanced to the stage of science.[2]

The pure scientist is quite convincing in his need for "figures" and yet a poet, in this case Philip James Bailey in 1839, could offer a counter plea for the importance of "feelings":

> We live in deeds, not years; in thoughts, not breaths;
> In feelings, not figures on a dial.[3]

THE QUANTITATIVE APPROACH

The scientific method is based upon the natural science model that assumes quantitative measurement, methodological rigor, and the derivation of replicable facts. In general, this approach begins with a hypothesis generation stage in which various causal or consequential relationships are defined. The researcher then produces data by counting and measuring things. Subsequently, the hypotheses are accepted or rejected on the basis of statistical analyses of the resulting data.

It is obvious that this approach is well suited to the basic research of the physical sciences. Hypotheses are usually based on a well defined theoretical framework of general laws, data can be gathered in a rigidly controlled setting and results can be analyzed with impartial quantitative methods. Finally, the test can be repeated numerous times. This traditional approach has been adopted by the social sciences and operationalized in several forms: (1) the experimental method in psychology associated with behaviorist theory; (2) survey research involving population samples, questionnaires, and structured interviews in consumer research; and (3) combinations of experimental and statistical treatments in psychology and social psychology.[4] The case for this approach is based on several arguments. First, it is noted that an objective perspective on the part of the researcher results in data which are impartial. Second, the notation system used to describe the world is produced by assigning numbers to objects. As such the description is more accurate information in that it provides a clearer, more distinctive picture of the world. And finally, the numbers used to describe objects result in systems which can be compared and reported. The points are well taken.

In marketing, the adoption of quantitative research approaches has been fueled primarily from two different sources. First, within the greater academic community, marketing has striven for legitimacy by promoting itself as a science. The natural science model and its accompanying procedures have been embraced by many marketing academics *and practitioners*—"Numbers have a comforting universality to brand managers justifying decisions up the organizational hierarchy . . ."[5] Secondly, the incredible advancement of computer hardware and software has made "number crunching" an easy, accessible way of analyzing large quantities of data. Leo Bogart, the general manager of the Newspaper Advertising Bureau, recently described the major developments in advertising research—one being the impact of computer technology:

> The computer was already around 15 or 20 years ago, but it was off in a back room and, like a caged beast, it had to be approached warily and only by trained keepers. As terminals spread to almost every desk in the agency, it becomes increasingly possible for everyone to access the vast amounts of marketing data stored on mainframes and to manipulate them in relation to possible alternative strategies.[6]

In combination these two sources have produced a significant impact. To illustrate, a survey that asked operating managers, research managers and research suppliers from a sample of American Marketing Association members what techniques they "used frequently" produced the results shown in the table on page 22.

The frequent use of quantitative techniques attests to the fact that such an approach to gathering or analyzing data is useful to researchers. In fact, in many instances a quantitative approach is not just useful but may very well be the only way. For example, in order to measure the effectiveness of an advertising campaign (management problem), change data needs to be calculated. Monsanto used a survey (research technique) in order to generate quantitative measures (information) of advertising effectiveness.[7]

Trial and Use of Thirteen Techniques by User Type
Used Frequently ("Use")

Technique	Operating Managers	Research Managers	Research Suppliers
Demographic segmentation	54.9%	64.1%	72.0%
Usage segmentation	52.0	59.9	68.6
Time-series analysis	43.4	45.2	27.8
Focus groups	35.4	51.1	62.3
Formal experiments	24.6	36.6	45.9
Psychographics	12.7	22.3	37.9
Response models	10.6	10.6	7.0
Computer simulation	10.1	8.7	6.5
Cluster analysis	5.2	7.7	16.5
Conjoint analysis	4.8	3.8	11.7
Multidimensional scaling	4.3	7.0	15.7
Bayesian analysis	4.2	1.5	2.2
Factor analysis	3.8	12.4	23.6[8]

Early in 1978, Monsanto rolled out its Chemical Facts of Life campaign. Its purpose was to eradicate "chemophobia," which Monsanto defined as the irrational fear of chemicals. The corporate campaign tried to create a balanced perspective regarding chemicals because of a poor industry image. To improve public attitudes and dispel bad publicity, Monsanto's campaign stressed that chemicals are both vital and necessary. Print and TV advertising emphasized Monsanto's concern about safe chemical use.

Approximately 800 telephone interviews were conducted with adults in each of four surveys during February, 1978 (pre); November, 1978 (post); December 1979 (post); and December, 1980 (post). The purpose of this research was to track what effect the campaign had on both the general public's and the target audience's (i.e. college graduates with income above $15,000) attitudes toward chemicals.

| Chemical Attribute | % Favorable or in Agreement | | | | Change 2/78—12/80 (3 years) |
	2/78 Pre	II/78 Post	12/79 Post	12/80 Post	
General opinion of chemicals	52%	54%	58%	53%	+1%
Chemicals have improved standard of living	76	80	82	85	+9 *
Chemicals adv. on balance, outweigh disadvantages	67	69	72	72	+5 *
Chemicals are beneficial to man	76	80	80	84	+8 *
Chemicals are necessary to life	58	66	61	68	+10*

* Statistically significant at .95 level.

The conclusions from this tracking study were "The Chemical Facts of Life" (CFOL) and Dupont's campaign made a definitive positive contribution in affecting better attitudes toward chemicals and the chemical industry during the past three years. CFOL accounted for a strong gain in the publics' awareness of Monsanto." The need to determine the effectiveness of an advertising campaign necessitates a definitive baseline. Only a quantitative approach to attitude measurement could have provided Monsanto with the information to derive an understanding of the relative change in attitudes towards chemicals.

Quantitative approaches, in general, are both useful and necessary to the marketing and advertising functions. But the strengths should be viewed in relationship to the accompanying weaknesses. What follow are the critical problems that are associated with quantitative approaches in marketing and advertising.

The Mystique of Quantity

There is a decided tendency to respond to numbers as though they were the repositories of occult powers; that the exactness of a figure equates to validity, to truth.

> The mystique of quantity is an exaggerated regard for the significance of measurement, just because it is quantitative,without regard either to what has been measured or to what can subsequently be done with the measure.[9]

There seems to be a certain comfort in numbers, a sense of security which exudes from a thick printout of crosstabs. As such, being able to state that two factors are significantly different, even if the difference is only slightly better than chance, seems to alleviate the researcher of any responsibility or insight. The numbers speak for themselves.

> Today by playing games with the data, we can construct impressive statistical artifacts. These may or may not have any relationship to the thinking or behavior of the human beings who were interviewed in the first place, but from the crucial criteria of their unintelligibility and the amount of awe and mystery they evoke, they can be very impressive indeed.[10]

Measuring What is Intended

The adoption of the scientific model has created an exaggerated concern for issues of reliability—the degree of consistency obtained from the devices we commonly employ: experimentation, survey research. In fact, it has been suggested that the cumulative nature of science requires a high degree of consensus among scientists and leads to an inevitable enchantment with problems of reliability.[11] In contrast, the problem of validity, or measuring that which one intends to measure, has been unconciously pushed into the background.

> We concentrate on consistency without much concern with what it is we are being consistent about or whether we are consistently right or

wrong. As a consequence we may have been learning a great deal about how to pursue an incorrect course with maximum precision.[12]

This particular shortcoming is evident in the recent example of a sportswear manufacturer. The company was interested in the reasons why people participated in sports. The secondary data and paper-and- pencil survey tests seemed to reconfirm the same notion that competition, physical fitness and socialness were the key factors involved. While the results of these quantitative data were extremely reliable, further research was done with individual depth interviews to probe on the "feeling" involved when participating. After analyzing the interviews, it was concluded that reasons such as fitness or socialness were initial factors but that the reason for continuing was the feeling of "accomplishment." That is, the sense of accomplishment deriving from physical improvement was the driving force behind participation in sports. The quantitative data, while interesting and useful, was only able to define "what got them started." The management problem, however, was related to their ongoing participation.

In short, our mystique of quantity ties in with the neglect of issues relating to validity. We seem happy to pursue large samples of respondents with scaled attitude surveys. Having punched up the data we submit it to a statistical program that results in nice, neat columns of numbers. We may even continue the process by using that output (perhaps frequency data) as input into complex multivariate programs. Eventually, we proudly display our results with a certain assurance that we have nailed down our facts. However, it does not really much matter how sophisticated one gets in measurement techniques if the thing you are trying to measure keeps on escaping!

Artificial Categories

The quantitative approach, whether it involves counting cans on a shelf, income statistics, or consumer attitudes, typically involves the use of structured categories. The object to be measured is approached by the researcher who has a framework in mind; a standardized format. For example, we could ask an individual to respond to the questions: Would you rate Chrysler Motor Company as being:

progressive ___ ___ ___ ___ ___ ___ ___ conservative
              1   2   3   4   5   6   7

OR

Vice President George Bush is an excellent choice for president.

Agree very strongly	____
Agree fairly strongly	____
Agree	____
Undecided	____
Disagree	____
Disagree fairly strongly	____
Disagree very strongly	____

In both cases a response structure has been imposed on the individual. We have asked them to tailor their responses to our categories.

While such structuring may be reasonable in many cases, the problem is that people are not simple and straightforward; it can be difficult to fit them into categories and make them stay there. Human emotion and behavior is a complex, messy business although we sometimes forget exactly how messy. For example, at one recent research presentation the results of a consumer study was explained in terms of several empirically derived factors. The presenter calmly, almost proudly, proclaimed an R-value (a measure of association) attached to these factors of .4; and no one in the audience made a peep. The categories and analysis had managed to explain a mere 16 percent of the variance. That leaves *only* 84 percent of the behavior unexplained.

On the other hand, consumer behavior can be extremely simple and intuitively obvious but we persist in generating artificial categories. Let me illustrate the point. In a study for a small ice cream retailer, a questionnaire was prepared to be used in "intercept fashion" as individuals were entering the stores. The research design called for the interviews to be done both at the client's stores and a major competitor's. The researchers used a semantic differential format of fifteen dimensions to describe the product (including such bipolar adjectives as natural-artificial, heavy-light, very sweet-not very sweet). In comparing the client's product with the competition, however, there seemed to be no discernible pattern; the results were confusing, appearing to be almost random in nature. In a series of depth interviews it became apparent that people, for the most part, did not think in terms of creaminess or sweetness. In fact, most of the purchasing behavior could be explained in terms of simple situational factors (e.g., outside temperature, time of day). The quantitative survey broke things down into little units, not so much because the subjects thought in little units, but because that was the framework adopted by the researchers. The results, of course, were merely answers to questions.

Therefore, one of the consequences of the scientific approach is to think of people in Cartesian terms, as essentially rational, structured and well-behaved. It is a decided mistake:

> ...there are some human (and therefore consumer) needs and emotions—love, for example, and loyalty, and humor—which, because they are characterized by such variety of unconscious as well as conscious drives and influences, cannot be quantified. Attempt to do so, and the result is more a Frankensteinian parody of 'understanding consumers' than a working concept of the feelings of real human beings.[13]

THE QUALITATIVE APPROACH

There are many different terms or labels that are applied to the general quantitative approach which is used in social sciences research. The term "scientific method" is also roughly equivalent to objectivism, empiricism, or positivism. Of course, more important than the label is the notion that this approach is defined by a rigid set of characteristics which were discussed earlier. In large part, the most important characteristics we are concerned with are:

1. A deductive procedure—going from the top down using definitive preconceptions to formulate hypotheses.
2. Objective researchers—who remain detached from the phenomena under study.
3. Quantitative data—a researcher-imposed set of categories.
4. Statistical examination—using numbers to describe or predict amounts or relationships.

This approach, with its origins in the physical sciences, has been shown to be uniquely suited to predicting and understanding the inert or unemotive phenomena which such *scientists* encounter. Unfortunately, social scientists and marketing practitioners have to deal with an unruly, unstable object of analysis: the human being.

The roots of modern day qualitative research in marketing and advertising can be found in anthropology and sociology as practiced in the early part of this century. Their emphasis on human culture and interaction necessitated an approach which allowed the phenomena to be described in individuals' own natural language. The general approach which evolved, called Phenomenology, stood in direct contrast to the characteristics of the Scientific Method. For example, the traditional empiricist sets up preconceived realities which he or she seeks to test; the qualitative researcher begins with the data and inductively forms conclusions to fit that data. The procedure is from the bottom up, with the researcher attempting to reduce preconceptions of subject to a minimum.

By beginning with specific observations and building toward general patterns, the researcher is able to develop an understanding of the situation as it emerges from the data. Another contrast is the qualitative commitment to study people as a process of discovery. Detachment or strict objectivity on the part of the researcher is replaced by a need to get close to the data:

> The basic position of this orientation is that in order to understand social phenomena, the researcher needs to discover the actor's "definition of the situation"—that is, his perception and interpretation of reality and how these relate to his behavior. Further, the actor's perception of reality turns on his ongoing interpretation of the social interactions that he and others participate in, which in turn pivots on his use of symbols in general and language in particular. Finally, in order for the researcher to come to such an understanding he *must be able (albeit imperfectly) to put himself in the other person's shoes.*[14]

While a quantitative approach is based on a response framework created by the researcher, the qualitative approach is grounded in the language and symbols of the subjects; who becomes the expert about their world. The data consist of people's own written or spoken words as they define their world: "He lives there; he knows better than we do what it is like and how best to describe it." [15]

Qualitative methods allow us to know people personally and to see them as they are developing their own view of the world. The researcher has the opportunity to experience meaning in the form in which people feel it; to understand naturally occurring phenomena in their naturally occurring states.

And finally, it must also be mentioned that qualitative methods have the ability to provide a holistic view of a situation. That is, instead of measuring the parts of a situation by gathering data about isolated variables, scales, or dimensions, qualitative methods can result in a complete picture. The researcher may, then, be able to understand the totality, or the unifying nature of a particular setting.

> In contrast to experimental designs which manipulate and measure the relationships among a few carefully selected and narrowly defined variables, the holistic approach to research design is open to gathering data on any number of aspects of the setting under study in order to put together a complete picture of the social dynamic situation or program. [16]

It is evident that the qualitative approach displays a unique set of capabilities which place it in direct contrast to a quantitative approach. Each approach can "match up" with a particular problem situation to provide the best means for understanding. The Monsanto example, described earlier in this chapter, illustrated a typical scenario in which only quantitative measurement was appropriate. In the same regard, it is obvious that a qualitative approach may be the *only way* to gather data in another setting. The Laker Skytrain example provides a contrast because it represents another classic type of advertising problem—exploring individuals' beliefs.

> In 1980, Laker Skytrain was establishing itself in the North Atlantic run from London to New York. The fares were very low by comparison with the competition and were not yet matched by the major carriers except on a standby basis. Clearly price was a major choice determinant but it appeared to be difficult to separate low price from "no frills" or "cheap." Advertising research, carried out by D'Arcy-MacManus and Masius, was designed to identify the belief structure of various segments in the market for a transatlan-

tic seat. Using group discussions to generate information amongst the various segments, the resulting qualitative data were analyzed to determine the key beliefs that influence behavior.

The key summary belief that ran through all the other things they believed about Laker was a sense of obligation and gratitude towards Laker, but it appeared to be negated by a major "BUT" within Skytrain non users: "I think I should back Laker, but . . ." This negative part, the 'but,' related to the problem of consumers rationalizing the fare in their own minds. How could Laker do it at that price? Visions were of cutting corners, with Skytrain being perceived as being utilitarian, not to say spartan.

The belief model approach suggested a position that lay not so much in beliefs about Laker as in beliefs about the other carriers. Since they were believed to be following Laker's lead, the belief model helped to turn Laker's claim 'I give you everything they do but for a cheaper price' around to say 'Other airlines don't give you more, they just take more.' Thus potential customers, rather than asking Laker to explain his cheapness, were prompted to raise the question, at least in their own minds, as to why Pan Am, BA, or TWA charge more for the same service.[17]

The level of understanding needed to define a belief system is such that a structured format would not yield valid responses. This need to develop a thorough understanding of a set of concepts is also evident when marketers attempt to define a "consumption system." That is, to explain how people go about using a product or service. An an example, a large wine manufacturer recently decided to position a new product as a light, white wine aimed at a managerial/professional market. The initial idea for the TV advertising was to illustrate an individual walking in the door after work and having a drink—perhaps in the double martini stereotype. A series of group interviews illustrated the fallacy of this line of thinking. When respondents began to introspect on their behavior, it became apparent that they hardly every had a drink of any kind as soon as they came home. In fact, they really just wanted a short time to be alone; no dog, no kids. The qualitative research into consumption systems showed that it was only after "re-energizing" that the idea of having a drink become important.

The appropriateness of a qualitative research method, given the need to understand respondents' beliefs or consumption systems, is clearly evident in the Skytrain and wine examples. However, qualitative analyses, in general, are not a panacea; they are not without difficulties or limitations.

The Mystique of Quality

This mystique, like its counterpart, the mystique of quantity, also subscribes to the magic of numbers; only it views their powers as evil. One author goes so far as to see the magic of numbers as "a kind of black magic, effective only for evil ends, and seducing us into giving up our souls for what, after all, is nothing but dross."[18] This perspective is built on the belief that the understanding of human beings consists *only* of certain subjective essences which by their very nature are not quantifiable. Measurement, then, is pointless at best, and more than likely an impossible distortion of what is really important.

The key, of course, is that such extreme narrowness of thinking does not do justice to numerical description. Demography and economics, for instance, which are important disciplines that impact the study of human behavior, rely heavily on mathematical methods and quantitative specifications. While there is no single quantitative description which tells us everything about a particular phenomenon; it is equally true that there is no single qualitative description which is capable of imparting "total understanding" either. Certainly one of the greatest dangers in qualitative research is that some researchers and decision-makers naively profess that it contains the entire answer. It does provide us with an eminently useful perspective, but regretably it remains but one perspective of many.

Another way in which the mystique of quality works is the assumed prediction of behavior. A qualitative research technique may admirably succeed in obtaining a "true" attitude; however, such an attitude does not, necessarily, predict behavior.

A housewife interviewed in January may have the "true" opinion that she will buy a General Electric refrigerator in the summer. Her true motives may be the desire to get what she considers the best shelf arrangement. The stimuli presented during the interview, in the form of questions or discussion, lead only to responses denoting her preference for General Electric. Yet in August, when she decides to buy a refrigerator, she cannot withstand the temptation to shop around and look at a variety of brands. She will read the literature of different companies. Also, she will be exposed to different sales arguments in advertising and in the stores themselves. Cubic feet of space, shelf arrangements, and many other things will act as new stimuli on her. In the end, she will buy, say, a Frigidaire instead of a General Electric, and for reasons which were nonexistent in her conscious and unconscious mind at the time of the interview.[19]

In interpreting data that reflect the qualities of individuals expressed in their own language, there is a natural tendency to extend that "truth" beyond the situation; to other times and other conditions. Such universal applications can be a source of serious error with the qualitative researcher.

Over-Probing and Over-Interpretation

A much more subtle set of difficulties that can be present in qualitative research arises from two sources: the application of the techniques, and the interpretation of the resulting data. In the first situation, the researcher loses sight of the problem and, being focused on the technique, continues to pry and probe in order to generate more data. As was stressed in Chapter One, the technique and the application of it must be used in a manner that most efficiently resolves the research question. Without some knowledge of the relevance of the responses and the level of understanding which is of importance to the problem at hand, it is possible for a depth interview to result in an extended series of "Why?" questions. The respondent is being asked to justify and rationalize an action which may have no motivation; it may be instinctual, habitual, reflexive, or situational. What the researcher gets is merely answers to questions, reflecting more the eagerness of the subject to be a "good subject" than valid responses. Secondly, in analyzing data the researcher may overinterpret by attempting to derive a level of understanding or meaning which doesn't exist. It is similar to the anecdote about the young psychiatrist, who upon having been greeted by another individual with a cheery "Good Morning" is tormented by the thought of "What did he mean by that?" In analyzing qualitative data, researchers can "dig too deep" while endeavoring to generate knowledge of a situation. The result, of course, is an interpretation that may not be valid and which is certainly not relevant to a business decision.

Unrepresentativeness

Without question, the most difficult problem associated with qualitative methods is the unrepresentativeness of the resulting data. In most cases, the sample that is used in a qualitative study is small and is not derived from a probability sampling plan. As such, there are no means of assessing the chance or probability of the sample estimate being equal to the true population value. Without this assurance of the representativeness of the data, it becomes impossible to generalize to other settings or subjects. Qualitative research, then, allows the researcher to observe and understand general processes as they occur under specific conditions. The subject or his/her response cannot, therefore, be assumed to represent any larger population. Another source of unrepresentativeness that can be present in qualitative data is related to biases occurring within the researcher/respondent interaction. The researcher, approaching the respondent(s) without the categorization system which is mandatory with quantitative methods, is in the position of being able to collect and analyze data selectively. Such selectivity resembles a sieve which may strain the information according to the prejudices of the researcher.

MIXING AND MATCHING

Having explored the strengths and weaknesses of both quantitative and qualitative approaches, it is evident that our "fence sitter" is in the enviable position of being able to go with whichever strength is appropriate given the problem situation. With this understanding, the researcher can develop creative research designs which, when necessary, oscillate between the approaches in order to derive data that are real, deep and hard. The final portion of this chapter deals with research designs which contain more than one data-generating approach. As such, they represent more complex problem situations in which the reliance on a single approach or technique may not be appropriate.

Qualitative then Quantitative

The most widely accepted application of qualitative marketing research is in situations in which it is linked to a quantitative approach. Specifically, even extreme "figures" people have recognized the usefulness of qualitative data in a pre-quantitative, provisional role. In this situation, the qualitative approach is not meant to stand alone, but rather is used in an exploratory fashion. This exploratory approach can take one of several different forms. Probably the most prevalent form of exploratory research is to use qualitative data to generate ideas or hypotheses which will be tested in a quantitative setting. The Balfour example below is just such a qualitative-quantitative arrangement.

A leader in the field of "employee recognition" products, Balfour recognized the need to understand fully the market and the desires of the end users. A comprehensive, multiphase study was conducted in which the first phase was designed to determine attitudes, policies, and practices involving employee recognition and to transfer that information into testable hypotheses. Data were generated in a series of focus-group sessions and in-depth personal interviews among personnel administrators in 16 major cities with over 200 companies participating. Several key hypotheses were developed out of the qualitative phase:

1. Traditional service awards are not highly meaningful to employees and do not sufficiently convey corporate appreciation.
2. Recognition itself is more important than the award; that awards for achievement and accomplishment on the job mean more than do chronological service awards alone, and that personnel administrators know that there is a need for recognition.
3. Personnel administrators are not entirely confident that their programs are sufficient; they need and want guidance and a full-service approach from suppliers.

The quantitative phase of the study entailed a self-administered questionnaire which elicited responses from 346 personnel administrators. The questionnaire was highly structured and specifically designed to generate projectable, quantitative results in order to confirm or reject the stated hypotheses.[20]

While the Balfour example illustrates the manner in which qualitative research is used to generate testable hypotheses, qualitative research can also be employed in a much different manner. At times researchers need direction in terms of specifying certain operational aspects of anticipated quantitative research. As such, information can be generated via qualitative approaches to determine the form of the subsequent research. For example, in-depth interviews are useful for "pilot testing" a survey instrument. The questions used in the interviews are generated along the lines of the major issues involved in questionnaire construction and the subject (oftentimes an expert on the topic) is asked to evaluate the questionnaire in terms of such criteria. For example:

Decisions About Question Content

1. Is this question really needed?
2. Is this question sufficient to generate the needed information?
3. Can the respondent answer the question correctly?
4. Will the respondents answer the question correctly?

5. Are there any external events that might bias the response to the question?

Decisions Concerning Question Phrasing

1. Do the words used have but one meaning to all the respondents?
2. Are any of the words or phrases loaded or leading in any way?
3. Are there any implied alternatives in the question?
4. Are there any unstated assumptions related to the question?
5. Will the respondents approach the question from the frame of reference desired by the researcher?

Decisions Concerning the Question Sequence

1. Are the questions organized in a logical manner that avoids introducing errors?

Decisions on the Layout of the Questionnaire

1. Is the questionnaire designed in a manner to avoid confusion and minimize recording errors?[21]

The resulting opinion data are used to redesign the instrument to make it more consistent with the way the respondents think about the subject matter. The finished product, it is hoped, is more reflective of the target populations' point of view than the instincts of the researcher.

A final situation in which qualitative research may be a valuable exploratory tool is in the definition or clarification of a problem situation. For example, in one industrial product setting, management wanted to develop strategies for the allocation of resources among several elements of the communications mix. While the goal was related to resource allocation, the more immediate problem was to clarify the information-seeking behavior of purchasing agents. A focus group of purchasing agents was used to compile a list of frequently used information sources, including trade journal articles, technical experts and others. Such subjective information was then used in conjunction with a standard classification of buying tasks (new buy, straight rebuy, modified rebuy) in a large quantitative study of purchasing agents. Specifically, the respondents were asked to match up the information sources and the buying tasks in order to derive a numerical, projectable understanding of the relationship between sources and tasks.

In general, then, it is both appropriate and prudent to use a qualitative approach in anticipation of quantitative research. The linkage is particularly useful at stimulating the researcher into thoughtful considerations based upon subject-derived information. As such, the combination can nullify the critical problems involved in quantitative research. The difficulties involved in the derivation of researcher-defined categories, for example, can be minimized by using qualitative research to help generate the categories. Additionally, by clarifying a problem situation prior to a quantitative study, there is greater probability that the numbers will measure what they intend to measure; that increased understanding on the part of the researcher will be reflected in a more valid instrument.

Quantitative then Qualitative

While the quantitative-qualitative situation is not as prevalent as the more standard exploratory research, it nonetheless has an important similarity. Both extend the researcher's understanding of a phenomenon by exploring the interrelationship of the qualitative and quantitative approaches.

One important way in which quantitative research can precede qualitative is when survey methodology is used to identify the general characteristics of a phenomenon, as in most segmentation studies. The resulting quantitative description presents a necessary, though limited, meaning to the topic under study. Qualitative research can then be used to "flesh out" the description by humanizing the data in a manner that quantitative description cannot do. In such a way Western Union was able to develop a new service targeted towards the college market.

In a series of studies of the college market, Western Union became aware of the fact that college students had more money than ever before and spent it on quite a list of items besides tuition, room and board. The nation's 11.5 million students had $20 billion in discretionary income, which amounted to $175 monthly. One-third owned credit cards, 41% took a domestic airline trip in the previous year, 12 percent traveled abroad, 69 percent own stereo equipment, 75 percent own hand-held calculators and 92 percent own sports equipment. While such information on this market segment helped describe a certain aspect of behavior (the What and How much?), it didn't address the question of How?

Qualitative research examined the consumption patterns of the segment. Results indicated that while students have adequate income, they frequently did not plan their financial purchases. With little, if any, precautionary funds they were often caught short of money. The college market, then, while being large and active, also exhibited a significant problem in terms of financial planning. The resulting Western Union Charge Money Order Service addressed this problem with a service targeted specifically for the college market.[22]

Qualitative research can also be used after quantitative in an *explanatory* role. That is, the subjective data are used to interpret or give meaning in a situation in which the numbers are not sufficient for understanding. For instance, a large sport shoe manufacturer engaged in a quantitative survey to help define the nature of their customers. The results indicated a substantial percentage of the consumers were older women. A qualitative study was then undertaken to go beyond the numbers and find out why and how this segment consumed the product.

An additional way in which quantitative research is used prior to qualitative is when researchers have developed a longitudinal study to measure change over time. The most common manner in which this is done is with retail consumer panels that are representative samples of individuals or households from the population being studied. The data are collected from the same sample of respondents in regular intervals. The information generated enables the researcher to record a dynamic profile of consumer characteristics and activity. While it should be obvious how valuable panel data could be, it is equally obvious that plotting trends, measuring purchase frequency, eliciting competitor purchasing activity, and so on, does not provide a researcher with the "whole picture." For example, the following analyses are somewhat typical of panel data:

• Purchases by size of pack;
• quantity of the product bought on each occasion;
• day of the week on which purchases are made;
• price consciousness by demographic groups; and
• the relationship of quantity of purchases to size of household.[23]

Given these kind of data, qualitative approaches are often useful in exploring or interpreting the meaning behind changes or trends. If, for example, our panel shows that the size of package purchased is related to the time of year, we have no idea as to why this may occur. Various qualitative techniques could explore the "whys" of such occurrences.

Validation

There has been concern in the social sciences that results derived from certain methods reflect the unique characteristics of the *method*, as well as the trait or phenomenon under investigation. The notion is that no single measure is, or can be, a perfect indicator of human activity. Instead, additional methods should be used to ensure that the variance which is measured reflects that of the trait or characteristic, not the method. By using multiple methods it is possible to increase our confidence in our findings by generating differing viewpoints.

The validation use of qualitative research is particularly appropriate when it is used in combination with quantitative results. It can provide the researcher with two conceptually and operationally different ways of measuring the same thing. A research design developed by A. T. Cross illustrates how a qualitative technique can be used to verify and extend quantitative results.

The A.T. Cross Company is a major international manufacturer and marketer of writing instruments. In June of 1982, Cross initiated a study to provide insight into consumer preferences of various styles of Cross pen and pencil desk sets. Specifically, Cross wished to determine the preference among various product attributes: for example, 10-karat gold filled versus chrome writing instruments; cherry versus open-grained walnut bases; and centered versus off-centered writing bases.

A series of focus groups were conducted in which consumer preferences were explored. In contrast to standard focus groups that involve unstructured discussions, however, the groups were given specific, individual tasks to perform. The tasks involved tradeoff analysis, in which the members were asked to rate their preference for 20 pairs of desk sets. Having obtained "hard" data from the ranking process, the groups reverted to the more traditional method of conducting focus-group research. The moderator explored the preferences of individual members by comparing and contrasting each member's position with regard to the various decision alternatives.[24]

The ranking task and quantitative analysis (conjoint) resulted in a certain kind of understanding of preferences based upon a researcher-imposed measurement instrument. The validation of such responses was provided by an open discussion of the individuals' decision logic. By asking them to defend their choices in a group session, the strength and precision of their choice pattern could be analyzed. This is a luxury which would not have been possible if the analyses (quantitative and qualitative) had been performed on an either/or basis.

Programmatic Research

A final example of qualitative/quantitative integration can be illustrated in terms of programmatic research. "Programmatic" means that individual studies are generated out of previous studies, to build on the base of findings and extend understanding. Oftentimes it is appropriate to use different approaches at the various stages in order to take advantage of the unique capabilities of some techniques or to avoid the limitations of other techniques. From a comprehensive viewpoint, each study design is derived from the objectives of the research and the extent and manner in which previous findings met those objectives. The Zales example is a perfect illustration of a research program that oscillates between both qualitative and quantitative approaches.

The Zale Corporation has about 1500 stores operating in the United States and abroad; sales in 1981 topped more than $828 million. As such, Zales is the world's largest jewelry retailer with approximately 7 percent market share of national sales. In 1978 Zales began a research effort that entailed five studies over a 3-year period.

February, 1978—National Jewelry Profile: Zales, being a newcomer to consumer research, decided to get initial data about the industry and the jewelry customer in general. Surveys were mailed to 40,000 American households (with 27,000 returns). The questionnaire provided a quantitative baseline on jewelry purchases made during the past year. Questions included the number of items purchased, type of jewelry, who made the purchase, how much they paid, and where they bought it.

December, 1978—Consumer Attitudes: To provide a better view of the market, a second study focused on consumer purchases and attitudes. The study consisted of two phases. A destination study was conducted at a sample of Zales locations where respondents were intercepted leaving the store and asked questions regarding where they had been prior to their Zales visit, where they were going afterwards, how many were in their party, what they were shown, and what they bought. The questions were constructed in both a categorical framework and open-ended. An attitudinal phase of purchasers and nonpurchasers was conducted with a follow-up telephone survey of cooperative respondents to the destination study. The respondents were asked a number of in-depth questions regarding their jewelry shopping habits and their visits to Zales.

February, 1980—Quantitative Competitive Attitude: Approximately 400 interviews were conducted in respondents' homes among men and women 18 years and older in Atlanta, Houston, Kansas City and San Diego. The study's main objective was to obtain information pertaining to consumer awareness and attitudinal perceptions of both Zales and key competition in the four markets.

March, 1980—Consumer Motivation: In 57 in-home, personal interviews in Dallas, Philadelphia and San Francisco, respondents were asked to discuss the motivation underlying their jewelry purchases. The results revealed the extent of the emotional risk of the purchase, the customers' lack of standards by which to compare and evaluate merchandise, and the importance for the customer to feel reassured in every possible cue he/she gets from the store and its advertising. When making a major jewelry purchase, the customer looks for four things—value, reliability, selection and style.

February, 1981—Message Evaluation: After completing the consumer research, the final step was to find out just what *says* value, reliability, selection and style. 40 words, phrases and sentences were developed; each was then tested to measure emotional response, recall, the importance of the attribute described, believability, and its appropriateness for Zales. Respondents viewed these phrases on a TV screen and were monitored by an electrodermal response device. Also, animatics, or "cartoonized" versions of commercials, provided a vehicle for testing each commercial in terms of its impact; whether it communicated the proper message, if it motivated the respondent, and whether it differentiated Zales from other jewelry stores.[25]

The long-run vision of Zales research design enabled the researchers to conduct each study within the context of the previous research. This process resulted in each research component building on strengths and compensating for weaknesses of prior research. It is an oscillating procedure, going back and forth using different approaches and techniques to achieve overall understanding of the phenomenon in question. The approach is similar to the example of the paleontologist detailed at the end of Chapter One. With a goal firmly established, research efforts proceed incrementally, with each problem stage being identified as a separate unit. The paleontologist uses vastly different tools to yield information at different levels of analysis; the sledge hammer to attack large chunks of matter and a stereoscopic microscope to derive minute understanding of a phenomenon. The practical marketing and advertising researcher must be equally prepared to define long-run objectives and then build research designs in a creative manner, thereby yielding information of a comprehensive nature.

FINALITIES

Understanding Bob and Sally

The dichotimization of researchers into "figures" people and "feelings" people is an unfortunate reality. Individuals seem to become comfortable with one approach, with a certain set of techniques, and consequently view a research problem from a very structured mind-set. While each approach has it strength and weakness, the danger lies in the kind of exclusive preoccupation with one method that leads to a systematic neglect of the uniqueness of another. This limited focus perpetuates the division.

  Perhaps there is a certain amount of self-importance attached to marketing and advertising researchers—and their techniques. Perhaps we need to remind ourselves that the rationale for doing consumer research is based upon the notion that the consumer can tell us things; information that will help reduce the risk of decision-making. Technique choice is secondary to matching "opinion" to "problem." Perhaps we need to start at the beginning and ask ourselves the question **"Does the marketing research community really believe that each consumer's opinion counts?"** In a recent editorial, one professional researcher provided a different perspective to this basic question:

> Consider how each researcher might answer that question if he or she were questioned in conventional research ways. Consider how ludicrous researchers might seem if they applied their typical fieldwork modes to normal human interactions:
>
> **Bob to Sally:** "I'd like to get to know you better. I'll phone you to administer a 10-minute interview consisting largely of structured descriptive questions. I'll also have you rate intentions on a five-point rating scale and briefly explain your rating. If this works out, I'll then expedite our dialogue by having a machine ask you questions on the telephone. Maybe to save money, I'll mail you self-administered check-off questionnaires instead."
>
> **Sally to Bob:** "Come on, you call such straight-jacketing of my thoughts being interested in what I think? I really want to know all

about you—your opinion counts—so let's get personal. I'll intercept you in the local shopping mall and query you for 15 minutes, asking you structured and semi-structured descriptive and appraisal questions which will really tell me where you're at!"

Bob to Sally: "You ask me a handful of mostly close-ended questions when I'm busy shopping and assume you'll understand me as a complex, changing human being? I can think of a better way. I'll sit you in a room with ll other people and watch behind a one-way mirror. With a skillful focus-group moderator, your life, your dreams, your aspirations, your attitudes will come clearly into view. God, I'm an empathetic person!"

Sally to Bob: "Some empathy. My share of the group's talking time will be seven minutes, if I'm lucky. Let's face it, none of these communications formats can produce important understandings about one another. Let's forget about discourse. Since our opinions really count, let's set up experiments. I'll array some test objects in front of you and record your reactions. Then you'll do the same. It'll cost very little, and over time we'll be able to track one another's behavior and develop mathematical formulas to predict what one is likely to do in the future. Ideally, we'll develop such powerful modeling equations that we won't even have to talk to one another any more. We'll then have that warm feeling that comes from knowing that we really value each other's opinions!"

Bob to Sally: "Real nice . . . and so scientific. Isn't it wonderful that we're such caring and sharing people."[25]

Managerial Insights

While Bob and Sally's dialogue may be a bit arcane, the concept is entirely relevant: Are we really prepared to do what is necessary to understand people in their consumptive roles? This chapter has shown that quantitative and qualitative approaches have unique capabilities, and that the thoughtful choice of an appropriate technique will result in increased value of the information. In retrospect it can be noted that such a choice is based upon three critical issues:

43

Understand The Underlying Philosophies. This is not referring to simply the ability to generate and interpret a regression coefficient or how to moderate a focus group. Instead, knowledge should be in terms of the elementary assumptions of each approach—or the philosophy of the Scientific Method and Phenomenology. It is this fundamental knowledge of the approaches that will ultimately direct the researcher in the construction of an appropriate research design. Without such an appreciation, the tools take on a decidedly mechanistic flavor.

Seek Counter-balancing Strengths. Strengths should be used to compensate for weaknesses. The methods used in a study should reflect the result of a mental inventory on the part of the researcher in which a review of the advantages and disadvantages of specific techniques is undertaken. The use of multiple methods in a research design should not, therefore, be perceived as a luxury. In fact, many research problems exist at different levels of meaning and thus require a combination of research tools.

Appreciate Human Complexity. The human spirit is an incredible mix of frailties, egos, insecurities, biases, rationalizations, bravados, inconsistencies and irregularities. Much of what we know about people derives from asking them questions and faithfully recording their answers. But such knowledge is based upon surface-level understanding of a group of individuals, and then generalized to larger populations. Given that people exist at different personality levels, probing these levels will merely increase the difference between and among individuals. The resulting idiosyncrasies do not lend themselves to summative processes.

ENDNOTES

[1]Zelditch, Morris (1962), "Some Methodological Problems of Field Studies," *American Journal of Sociology*, (University of Chicago Press: Chicago), p. 566.

[2]Kelvin, William Thomson (1891-94), *Popular Lectures and Addresses.*

[3]Bailey, Philip James (1839), *A Country Town.*

[4]Diesing, Paul (1966), "Objectivism vs. Subjectivism in the Social Sciences," *Philosophy of Science*, 33 (March-June), p. 124.

[5]Lannon, Judie (1986), "New Techniques for Understanding Consumer Reactions to Advertising," *Journal of Advertising,* 26 (August-September), p. RC-6.

[6]Bogart, Leo (1986), "Progress in Avertising Research?" *Journal of Advertising Research*, 26 (June-July), p. 12.

[7]Monsanto Company: used with permission.

[8]Myers, John G., William F. Massy and Stephen A. Greyser (1980), *Marketing Research and Knowledge Development* (Prentice-Hall, Inc.: Englewood Cliffs), p. 211.

[9]Kaplan, Abraham (1964), *The Conduct of Inquiry* (Chandler Publishing Co.: Scranton), p. 172.

[10]Bogart, Leo (1986), "Progress in Advertising Research?" *Journal of Advertising Research*, 26 (June/July), p. 14.

[11]Merton, Robert K. (1957), *Social Theory and Social Structure* (Glencoe, Ill.: The Free Press), p. 448.

[12]Deutscher, Irwin (1966), "Words and Deeds: Social Science and Social Policy," *Social Problems*, 13, p. 241.

[13]R & D Sub-Committee on Qualitative Research (1979), "Qualitative Research—A Summary of the Concepts Involved," *Journal of the Market Research Society,* 21, p. 110.

[14]Schwartz, H. and J. Jacobs (1979), *Qualitative Sociology* (The Free Press: N.Y.), p. 272.

[15]Schwartz, H. and J. Jacobs (op. cit.), p. 7.

[16]Patton, M. (1980), *Qualitative Evaluation Methods* (Sage Publications: Beverly Hills), p. 40.

[17]D'Arcy - MacManus and Masius: used with permission.

[18]Kaplan, A. (1964), *The Conduct of Inquiry* (Chandler Publishing Co.: Scranton, Pa.), p. 206.

[19]Politz, Alfred (1957), "Science and Truth in Marketing Research," *Harvard Business Review*, 35 (January-February), p. 117.

[20]L.G. Balfour Company: used with permission:

[21]Tull, Donald and Del I. Hawkins (1984), *Marketing Research: Measurement and Method* (Macmillan: New York), p. 257.

[22]The Western Union Telegraph Company: used with permission.

[23]Parfitt, John (1978), "Panel Research" in *Consumer Market Research Handbook*, R. Worcester and J. Downham (eds.) (Van Nostrand Reinhold Co: N.Y.), p. 194.

[24]A.T. Cross Company: used with permission.

[25]Karger, Ted (1986), "Your Opinion Counts—Only if Researchers Really Listen," *Marketing News*, 20 (July), p. 2.

CHAPTER THREE

OBSERVATION METHODS

Observation methods have been developed and used for centuries in many diverse disciplines and can play a very important role in modern marketing and advertising research. The practicality of the approach should be readily apparent to anyone who is attempting to describe humans in their everyday activities.

For its Breyers ice cream account, the Young and Rubicam advertising agency wanted to get a taste of what ice cream really means to American consumers. First came traditional focus-group interviews. The market researchers decided to try something novel: They visited six families at home to observe ice-cream indulgence first hand. They photographed people lounging in their favorite chairs and taking that first scrumptious lick. They snooped in freezers, inspected bowls and utensils, watched people spoon on toppings and listened to one woman describe how she dims the lights and flips on the stereo before digging in. "We learned about people's emotional response to ice cream and found that it's a very sensual, inner-directed experience," says Robert Baker, marketing director for Breyers at Kraft Inc. "Hopefully, this extra research will guide the agency in developing more effective advertising." [1]

Observation methods are appropriate for describing consumption behaviors as they occur. In this regard, such methods are no different from survey methods or panel data that ask people what behaviors they engage in; the behaviors are public and conscious actions. The critical difference between observation and these other methods is that with observation we need not ask people to recall the action, nor do we rely on their own self-reports. The researcher observes and the subject merely engages in behaviors. This emphasis on the direct observation of behavior in everyday situations is an attempt to contruct basic understandings of human actions—even eating ice cream.

The important point is that we often begin to ask the question "Why?" before we thoroughly understand "How?" and "When?" We want to probe for explanations and rationalizations. Our researchers, managers, directors, VPs, and other experts assume that we already know everything there is to know about behaviors and we need to get on with the more serious and difficult task of explaining why those behaviors occured. The description of observable acts is a necessary, but often overlooked, component in consumer research. Perhaps that eloquent sportsman, Yogi Berra, said it best when he once remarked, "You can observe a lot just by watching."

WHAT TO OBSERVE

There is one major aspect of an observational study that must be defined before the specifics of "how to" are discussed—event definition. Event definition is the selection for observation of integral behavioral occurrences or events. An event can be a single act or a series of individual acts which have some importance as a larger behavioral unit (conflict resolution, walking down a grocery aisle, and so on). For example, the "cough" was the observational event identified by a theatre manager in a study to measure boredom or disinterest on the part of the audience:

> One cougher begins his horrid work in an audience, and the cough spreads until the house is in bedlam, the actors in rage, and playwright in retreat to the nearest saloon. Yet let the action take a turn for the better, let the play tighten up, and that same audience will sit in silence unpunctuated by a single tortured throat.[2]

The behavioral event was, in this case, a single act. The researchers focused on observing the "cough" as an alternative means of assessing the amount of boredom. There are many possible single act units that can be the basis for a behavioral observation study. For instance, physical distance has been used to understand the power hierarchy in the USSR by observing who stood next to whom in Red Square reviewing the May Day parade. Others have observed the diameter of a circle of children as an index of induced fear: "Although the diameter of the circle was about eleven feet at the beginning of the storytelling, by the time the last ghost story was completed, it had been spontaneously reduced to approximately three feet."[3] Several additional marketing-oriented examples (by Webb et al.) illustrate the diversity of possible studies and individual acts:[4]

> Radio-dial settings are being used in a continuing audience-measurement study, with mechanics in an automotive service department the data-gatherers (Anonymous, 1962). A Chicago automobile dealer, Z. Frank, estimates the popularity of different radio stations by having mechanics record the position of the dial in all cars brought in for service. More than 50,000 dials a year are checked, with less than 20 per cent duplication of dials. These data are then used to select radio stations to carry the dealer's advertising. (p. 39)

> A committee was formed to set up a psychological exhibit at Chicago's Museum of Science and Industry. The committee learned that the vinyl tiles around the exhibit containing live, hatching chicks had to be replaced every six weeks or so; tiles in other areas of the museum went for years without replacement (Duncan, 1963). A comparative study of the rate of tile replacement around the various museum exhibits could give a rough ordering of the popularity of the exhibits. (p. 36)

> Another procedure to test advertising exposure is the "glue-seal record" (Politz, 1958). Between each pair of pages in a magazine, a small glue spot was placed close to the binding and made inconspicuous enough so that it was difficult to detect visually or tactually. The glue was so composed that it would not readhere once the seal was broken. After the magazines had been read, exposure was determined by noting whether or not the seal was in tact for each pair of pages, and a cumulative measure of advertising exposure was obtained by noting the total number of breaks in the sample issue. (p. 44)

The single act is an important observational unit because it allows the observer to "zero-in" on a specific behavior; it enables one to count the frequency or the duration of an act. By focusing on a single activity, however, we may well have reduced our analysis to simply counting coughs or radio station settings. A more broadened perspective would result in an exploratory process in which single acts are less important than a composite of behavioral activities. The emphasis is not on defining individual acts or categories but rather the impressionistic observation of a stream of behaviors—ice cream indulgence for instance. One reported study was interested in determining the relative importance of location and brand in influencing consumer purchases of milk. The observation was done as follows:

> In order to study the actions of supermarket customers during their purchases of milk, an aluminum box was built around the motion camera and attached to the back of a nearby meat display case. The camera was located 4 feet above and 18 feet away from the milk display area. Its field of vision covered the entire display area. Thus arranged, the operation of the camera did not attract attention at any time during the study. To conserve film, the experimenter turned on the camera only when someone entered the aisle where the milk display was located.[5]

Such behavioral composites usually define an entire episodic event. In another example participant observation was used to study the impact of family group interaction on children's understanding of television advertising.[6] The researcher "joined-in" during periods of natural family group television viewing. "As such, episodes lasted until the child or some other member of the viewing situation redirected their activity or were redirected." This type of episodic or process observation provides the opportunity to investigate emerging patterns in a dynamic setting.

An additional issue that should concern the researcher when deciding "What to Observe" is dross rate. Dross can be defined as the data that are accumulated during interviewing or observing that are irrelevant to the topic at hand. The extreme example that has been used to illustrate "dross" is the use of an observation technique to study the reasons for railroad crossing accidents. Obviously, the infrequency of such accidents at any particular crossing would make observation a totally inefficient technique; irrelevant data could be gathered for months or years. The choice of "What to Observe" should, therefore, be determined by identifying data that are not important to the management problem. Irrelevant observations should be "squeezed out," resulting in a greater density of relevant data.

The amount of dross can be significant because the total amount of observational data that can be obtained in a short period is, at times, overwhelming. Given the fact that Barker and Wright have written a book entitled, *One Boy's Day* (a detailed account of activities of a 7-year old boy in a single day), it is evident that specificity can be a valuable asset in designing observational studies.[7] For example, in the supermarket study:

> The milk purchasing behavior could have been recorded from the time subjects entered the store. Instead, the researcher turned the camera on "when someone entered the aisle where the milk display was located."

In summary, there are three basic conditions that function as prerequisites to formal observation.[8] First, the *data must be accessible* to observation. We are interested in behaviors, in observable acts. Any interest in deriving various attitudes, opinions or motivations should be left to other kinds of research methods. A second basic condition is that the behavior should be *repetitive, frequent or otherwise predictable.* We must be able to define events in such a manner that our observations are timely and efficient. And finally, the event must *cover a relatively short time period.* A study that is designed to "observe" the entire decision-making process that a couple would go through in purchasing a new home could take several months, if not longer. These conditions can be satisfied over a wide range of events: the number of coughs, nods, tugs, glances or smiles; the time it takes to make a decision or to look at an advertisement; the order that a child plays with a group of toys; the manner in which an individual uses a new piece of machinery; or the way that a family eats ice cream.

HOW TO OBSERVE

There are many different ways to observe. We can eavesdrop or peek around corners; we can install cameras and tape recorders. We have the option of observing people or the physical evidence which they leave behind. One of the things that make observations such an exciting possibility is just this fact—the different ways to observe are numerous and require an imaginative, creative mind. In contrast to much of the survey work that is centered on "very satisfied . . . very unsatisfied" scales, deciding how to observe presents an intriguing set of options. With this in mind, this section is organized along the lines of the major options available to the researcher.

The first choice available to the researcher is the nature of the setting. The observation setting may be somewhere along a natural-artificial continuum. A completely natural setting is illustrated by the kind of observation conducted by an astronomer, a vulcanologist or the ethologist attempting to study the lives of animals in their natural habitat. In our situation, the natural setting is the world in which we live. We observe people as they do things in the environment in which they normally exist: in the supermarket, at the bank, in their homes, or while waiting for a bus. In contrast, Seymour studied the conflict resolution behavior of husbands and wives in a highly artificial setting.[9] Automobile purchasing was the object under investigation, but the subjects had written descriptions of the automobiles, and they were confined to a room with a one-way mirror.

The advantage of such an artificial setting is that we are able to control extraneous influences that may adversely influence the behavior we are attempting to observe. For example, since the conflict resolution study was focused on husbands and wives, it would have been a problem if the study couldn't control outside influences (such as relatives, friends, or salesmen). There are several additional reasons to consider the artificial (or contrived) setting:

> The researcher need not wait for events to occur, but rather instructs the participants to engage in the needed kind of behavior. This means that a great many observations may be made in a short period of time; perhaps an entire study can be completed in a couple of days or a week. This can substantially reduce costs. The laboratory also allows the greater use of electrical and/or mechanical equipment than does the natural setting and thereby frees the measurement from the observer's selective processes.[10]

The obvious disadvantage is that the artificial setting can be highly reactive, altering the subjects' behaviors according to their interpretation of the rules and expectations of the surroundings. In general, it is advisable to try to maintain as much realism as possible in the immediate research environment in an attempt to minimize all the reactive biases that result from people being in "test" situations. Several large research firms, for instance, use mobile shopping units which they park in front of shopping malls or grocery stores. The inside of these mobile units are set up to resemble an actual store aisle. In this way the researcher can control the data gathering operation (e.g., who is tested, what stimuli they are exposed to). However, the subjects are people who are shopping, the surroundings are designed to be as realistic as possible, and the subjects are often allowed to keep what they "purchase."

One of the better examples of the natural versus artificial setting tradeoff is provided by Steve Barnett of Planmetrics Inc., a Chicago-based consulting firm. A group of electric utilities was interested in where people set their home-heating thermostats. The utilities previous fuel-use projections, based partly on poll takers' reports of customer interviews, were falling short of reality. According to Barnett:

> Your typical market-research interview is a highly artificial situation. You have an interviewer asking very specific questions to a stranger who, chances are, has given almost no previous thought to what he's being questioned about. The subject winds up giving the answers he thinks he's supposed to give. The results can be expressed in terms of neat percentages, but as a practical matter, they're almost useless.[11]

The results were quite different when Planmetrics installed TV cameras in the room where the thermostat was kept in 150 homes. "People might say they kept the things at 68 degrees, but it turned out that they fiddled with them all day. Older relatives and kids—especially teenagers—tended to turn them up, and so did cleaning ladies."

A second choice available to the researcher is the use of an experimental or a passive design. An experimental design entails the researcher specifying in advance the behaviors or cues that are important and then altering the environment so that these "treatments" can be specifically observed. For example, if we were concerned with the impact of shelf arrangement on the purchase of detergent, the different configurations could be altered between stores. An experimental design is appropriate when the researcher has determined *a priori* the specific behaviors that are to be observed. Given that set of specific behaviors or hypotheses, the researcher is in a position to manipulate the appropriate variables and to concentrate on those unique observations. By contriving the situation, key factors can be closely scrutinized in a timely, efficient manner, thereby minimizing the dross rate. For example, one researcher was interested in observing the nature of conformity in consumer behavior.[12] Subjects were asked to choose the best suit from among three identical suits. Confederates were used in different ways to offer their opinion prior to the subjects' choice. The contrived design enabled the researcher to manipulate differing conformity situations and study subjects' behavior.

In contrast to these experimental situations, the researcher might be more inclined to observe in a passive manner the data emerging from the situation. The researcher has no hand in manipulating the way in which the scenario is presented or preselecting which specific behaviors will be observed. The advantage of a passive design is that the researcher is able to discover certain elements or describe a process as it actually occurs. Such a discovery approach is described by one author as "watching and wondering" because it is open-minded, with no preconceived hypotheses being tested.[13] In a recent illustration a large regional bank was concerned with the problems of getting Automatic Teller Machines (ATMs) accepted and used by the public. The research design was an observational approach in which individuals were unobtrusively watched as they confronted the ATM. A specific discovery was that new ATM card recipients waited until no one else was in line before approaching the machine. This apparent fear of fumbling or appearing to be an ATM illiterate (which never surfaced in direct interviewing) was a significant deterent to card use. The passive design of the research allowed the researchers to observe in an exploratory mode, hoping that key factors would emerge from the data.

The next decision is concerned with the choice of observing people or the physical traces that people leave behind. In most situations consumer researchers go to the source for their information, the consumer. But there are situations where it is either inappropriate or impossible to observe people or ask them questions. An alternative is to observe the physical traces which survive from past behaviors. Perhaps the relevance of such traces was best illustrated by the singular Sherlock Holmes, who contributed to advances in forensic science by publishing monographs on the science of detection-by-observation. One of his initial works, *Upon the Distinction between the Ashes of the Various Tobaccos*, illustrated the differences among the 140 varieties of cigar, cigarette, and pipe tobacco. A later work entitled, *On the Tracing of Footsteps,* detailed the use of Plaster of Paris as a preserver of impresses.[14] Unfortunately, most consumer researchers have not exhibited any of the insightful or imaginative qualities of Mr. Holmes. But while such resourcefulness is infrequent, there have been a number of examples in marketing and advertising:

> Sawyer noted the problem of estimating liquor sales in Wellesley, Massachusetts, a city without package stores. Sawyer solved the problem by studying the trash carted from Wellesley homes, taking specific note of the number and variety of empty liquor bottles.[15]

> University of Arizona students spent 3 hours per week for 4 years sifting through garbage at the city dump. Among other conclusions, results showed that the average family wastes about 10 percent of the food it buys and that the middle class wastes more than either the rich or the poor.[16]

In fact, a number of potential uses for the analysis of physical traces (in this case, garbage) have been advocated by other consumer researchers:

1. Supplement current survey research data (i.e., under-reporting of beer consumption.
2. Market share estimates within specific groups.
3. Consumption rates within specific groups.
4. Consumption profiles of specific groups.
5. Consumer reactions to changes in the marketing mix.
6. Packaging and consumer efficiency.
7. Effectiveness of product sampling and direct mail campaigns (i.e., how many direct mail pieces are thrown away unopened).[17]

By studying traces, any bias or reactivity from asking people questions or knowing that they are being observed is totally minimized. In the museum example we could simply ask people, "Which exhibit did you enjoy the most?" or have them rate each exhibit on a seven-point scale from Very Interesting to Very Uninteresting. A camera could be used or an observer could be stationed near the exhibit in order to watch people's behaviors or eavesdrop on their conversations. In each of these approaches, however, there is a chance that subjects will alter their behavior knowing that they are the center of attention. As we've seen, they may forget, react negatively to the interviewer, pose for the camera, and so forth. The floor tiles, in contrast, just lie there. The data are collected on what people do, not what they say they do. As we have noted, many consumers portray themselves as they'd like to be rather than as they really are. For example, parents typically say they don't allow their children many treats, but a check of kitchen cupboards by consumer researchers usually turns up a wide range of goodies. While some people intentionally deceive, others just don't know. As one of our leading trash analysts recently noted, "Most people don't have any idea how many pounds of food they eat, and they usually claim they eat many more vegetables and fruits than they really do."[18]

One of the most fundamental distinctions that differentiate observational strategies concerns the degree to which the observer adopts an active role and becomes an integral part of the phenomenon being studied. The task of observation can be pursued along a participation continuum. On one extreme, the observer remains detached, separated from the activities being studied. In such a situation, the observer objectively reports what is seen; he is like Howard Cosell sitting in a booth high atop the stadium, describing the action of a football game. An alternative to this kind of description is to become a part of activities being investigated. The observer is immersed in the data as it occurs, and, as such, offers a very different view of the phenomena. George Plimpton, for example, described the nature of football in a book entitled *Paper Lion*. It detailed his exploits as he "became" a member of the Detroit Lions football team for two weeks. His description of football stands in stark contrast to that provided by the loquacious but, nonetheless, detached Mr. Cosell.

The advantages of participant observation are significant. The observer who remains detached in a physical sense will also be detached in an emotional sense: the description is separated from the feeling. Plimpton's description of football is enhanced by having experienced the physical punishment absorbed by a football player. The result is that the observer not only sees what is happening but feels it as well. The observer begins to share feelings, thoughts, intentions and meanings—a phenomenon known as "intersubjectivity."

Active participants and passive observers are distinguished by this concept. Participants are intersubjective, observers are not (with their subjects). Participants communicate *with* people; observers, if they do anything, do them *to* people. Participants can share ideas and values, and argue with and persuade; observers merely casually influence. Participants have intentions, observers predict. Participants endow others with *minds,* observers look only at the behaviour of *bodies.* Participants know *how* to do things, observers know *that* things are done.[19]

This intersubjectivity advantage is derived from the notion that inference is a natural extension of observation. Since observation and inference are difficult to separate, a key consideration in observational studies is how to make better inferences. By not being a part of the situation under study, the observer will necessarily infer on the basis of limited information. The outsider misses much of the significance of specific acts and may misinterpret some of what he or she does see. In contrast, the observer who participates in the events that are being investigated minimizes the psychological distance between observer and observed, thereby getting "closer" to the source of data. Inference is dissolved back into data collection as the observer directly experiences reality.

And finally, as intersubjectivity implies, the participant observer also has the advantage of experiencing the context in which observation takes place. Description is not just a sterile recounting of behavioral facts, but becomes a set of rich experiential impressions. Such impressions sensitize the observer to all the subtleties, contextual cues, and situational variables which may be important to understanding the situation under investigation.

A major disadvantage of high personal involvement is a direct result of its ability to minimize the distance between researchers and their subjects. Becoming involved in a situation may lessen the sharpness of observation, because researchers identify with the subjects and become accustomed to certain kinds of behavior. For example, Whyte reported that as he began the sociological investigation he detailed in *Street Corner Society,* everything he saw and heard was new and strange. He listened and watched intently. As he became part of the community (an active participant), the richness of the data increased, yet he found in himself an increased tendency to take for granted the sort of behavior he was observing.[20]

In conclusion, it should also be noted that one consumer research method is uniquely placed in the middle of the involved - detached continuum. "Protocol analysis" involves asking individuals to think out loud when solving a problem or engaging in a particular behavior. The subject is often followed by a researcher carrying a tape recorder or taking notes. As such, the researcher is involved in the process but only for purposes of data gathering (and remains detached from the specifics of the subjects' experiences). In addition, while the researcher is interested in a particular behavior, the verbalized thought is an excellent way to go beyond observable acts and to examine choice strategies, rationalizations and explanations: "Such protocols provide a richness of detail about the impact of the purchase environment—such as aisle promotions, shelf-facings and position, noise, or in-store-crowding—on consumer purchase decisions. The shopper's observations are collected as he or she moves through the store, up and down the aisles."[21] Excellent examples of these kind of data can be excerpted from a study by King:

Let's go this way, I think I need a little cleaner. Help me look for that Comet. That's in those pretty bottles, you know, for in the bathroom. The little kind. Ah! There it is. Let's get that aqua one.

Hey! I need some S.O.S. Pads too—just thought of it.

And I'd better get some waxed paper, because I've got to pack all that candy in wax paper. Let's see which is the cheapest around here. Uh-I think this Zee will do. That's pretty good. Think I'll keep going. I need some Kleenex. Hey! Do they mean this Springfield is on sale for 19 cents? Ooops! Well, I guess I dropped a few. (Laughter) Hey! Let's get about three of them. Say, how do you like those man-sized tissues? (Giggle) They should have a sample out so we could see it.

Oh, and let's get some of those napkins for the holidays. Huh? Hey! They've got two kinds, oh well. That's those holidays type.[22]

Finally, it should be evident that the amount of data collected through observation is potentially overwhelming. Watching a family in the act of purchasing a car can yield hundreds of behavioral cues in a matter of several minutes. In addition to the amount of data, there is the problem of separating the important data from the dross. In sum, the observer is faced with describing a complex stream of behavior and making some sense of it. The choices available to the researcher are to develop a coding system prior to observation, to apply a coding system after the behavior has occurred, or to describe the behavior in a qualitative, noncategorical manner. By using a behavioral code to guide the observation, the researcher has the advantage of focusing attention on a limited number of behaviors, consequently reducing the amount of data to be analyzed. A carefully developed category system provides a common frame of reference for observers and increases the likelihood that the relevant aspects will be accurately observed. But precoding assumes that the researcher knows which behaviors are important and, as such, is not appropriate for exploratory research. Secondary factors, subtle interactions and contextual cues can easily fall through the cracks between the behavioral codes.

If, however, the researcher chooses to observe without the aid of a categorization system, the option of coding the data after it has been gathered still remains available. The advantage to this is that a record of the event has been captured (i.e., either audio- or video-taped) and that the researcher can let the codes, or categories, emerge from the data. In addition, the complexities and intricacies are maintained which can provide for a richer description of the situation under study. But it should be noted that the postcoding process is time consuming and potentially unnecessary if the researcher knows exactly what behaviors are of importance to the study.

Finally, the advantages of foregoing any coding are consistent with those recounted throughout this book. Detailed descriptions and summaries do the best job of conveying the "sense" of the actual behavioral pattern. Subtleties, innuendoes, and inferences flow more readily from a description which is devoid of categories.

There are almost as many ways to systematize the process of observation as there are problem situations. Several different disciplines can be tapped to illustrate the range of categorization systems that have been used. A very general coding system is exemplified by the Flanders Interaction Analysis Categories for analyzing student/teacher interaction in the classroom:[23]

	Category Number	Description
	1	Accept pupils' feelings
	2	Praises or encourages pupils
Teacher Talk	3	Accepts pupils' ideas
	4	Asks questions
	5	Lectures
	6	Gives directions
	7	Criticizes/justifies authority
Student Talk	8	Student talk - narrow response
	9	Student talk - general response
	10	Silence or noise

By memorizing the code, the observer can easily transform the verbal activity in a classroom into a stream of numbers. In a similar manner, one researcher has noted the general categories that might be employed in observing a shopping trip. Several of the variables are as follows:

Shopping Trip Characteristics

Number of items purchased.
Number of items intended to purchase.
Time relative to number of items purchased.
Path through store.[24]

A more specific categorization system was developed by Robert Bales for describing the interaction of a group of people as it occurs, act by act. It has been used to observe conflict in an automobile decision-making task and to research marital roles in gift-giving.[25, 26] The categorization system is organized in the manner depicted in Figure 1:[27]

Figure 1 The Bales System of Categories for Recording Group Interaction

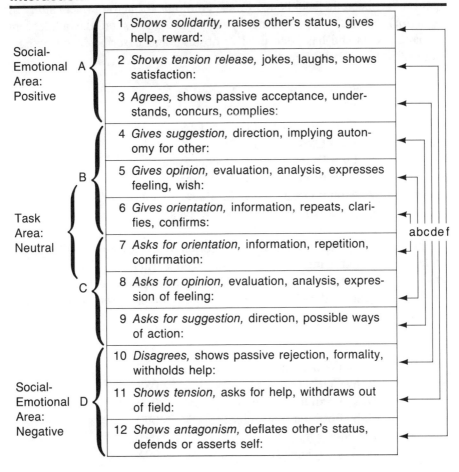

Social-Emotional Area: Positive	A	1 *Shows solidarity,* raises other's status, gives help, reward:
		2 *Shows tension release,* jokes, laughs, shows satisfaction:
		3 *Agrees,* shows passive acceptance, understands, concurs, complies:
Task Area: Neutral	B	4 *Gives suggestion,* direction, implying autonomy for other:
		5 *Gives opinion,* evaluation, analysis, expresses feeling, wish:
		6 *Gives orientation,* information, repeats, clarifies, confirms:
	C	7 *Asks for orientation,* information, repetition, confirmation:
		8 *Asks for opinion,* evaluation, analysis, expression of feeling:
		9 *Asks for suggestion,* direction, possible ways of action:
Social-Emotional Area: Negative	D	10 *Disagrees,* shows passive rejection, formality, withholds help:
		11 *Shows tension,* asks for help, withdraws out of field:
		12 *Shows antagonism,* deflates other's status, defends or asserts self:

a b c d e f

KEY:

a Problems of Communication
b Problems of Evaluation
c Problems of Control
d Problems of Decision
e Problems of Tension Reduction
f Problems of Reintegration

A Positive Reactions
B Attempted Answers
C Questions
D Negative Reactions

Behaviors can also be categorized on a very specific basis, focusing in on a whole range of unique activities. For example, the ethogram, a set of comprehensive descriptions of the characteristic behavior patterns of a species, has been the backbone of most ethological (the biological study of behavior) research. One coding system concentrates on the adolescent human species and has been used to observe and describe facial expressions of preschool children:[28]

1. Bared Teeth	9. Normal Face
2. Blink	10. Nose Wrinkle
3. Eyebrow Flash	11. Play Face
4. Eyes Closed	12. Pout
5. Grin Face	13. Pucker Face
6. Low Frown	14. Red Face
7. Mouth Open	15. Smile
8. Narrow Eyes	16. Wide Eyes

While consumer researchers have not gotten to this level of detail, there is at least one interesting exception. As noted earlier, the coding list for analyzing the garbage collected in the studies conducted at the University of Arizona generated 147 discrete, although perhaps messy, items.[29] For example:

Beer	086
Baby Food, Juice	087
Baby Cereal (pablum)	088
Baby Formula (liquid)	089
Baby Formula (powdered)	090
Pet Food (dry)	091
Pet Food (canned)	092
TV Dinners	093
Take Out Meals	094
Soups	095

All of the categorization systems presented thus far have been of the precode variety. That is, the observer systematically observes behaviors using the coding scheme to direct their attention or focus their energies on specific activities. The real tradeoffs evident in precoding or postcoding versus not employing any coding scheme are similar to the general arguments regarding quantitative versus qualitative research. The precoding focuses the researcher's attention (and minimizes dross) but in so doing imposes a set of categories on the data. Much of the subtlety and intricacy of the information is lost; the qualitativeness is forsaken and replaced by a smaller set of behavioral codes. Of course, such a reduced data set is useful if the researcher is interested in counting specific acts. If post-coding is done it allows the researcher to collect data in a more exploratory fashion, using the information itself to dictate the coding scheme. A full description of the event is best generated by avoiding any coding procedures and instead relying on unstructured observation to outline the behavioral patterns of the event.

Finally, it should be noted that there are devices commercially available to aid in the collection and analysis of observed behavior. For example, DataMyte Corporation manufactures hand-held, battery-powered microprocessors which enable the researcher to record behaviors in terms of frequency, duration, ratios between groups of behaviors, ranges and averages, and the sequential order of observations.

TRADE-OFFS

As with every other research technique that is described in this book, the observational approach has a unique set of strengths and weaknesses that should be considered. The following, then, are the major strengths that are related to "observation."

Strengths

The Actor's Point of View. The basis of qualitative research is found in the notion of minimizing the level of researcher-imposed thinking. Qualitative data are grounded in the symbols of the subjects as they define their own world. With observational methods, the observer shares in the activities of the individuals and is able to identify their perspective. Take, for instance, the engaging 1923 study and book done by Nels Anderson on *The Hobo*. It is an absolutely fascinating description of the everyday life of a hobo, based upon Anderson's keen observation as he traveled the railroads of this country. In the area of consumer behavior, a recent study was done for a large city's mass transit authority in which out-of-town visitors (subjects) were paid to use the subway system to get to different check points in a certain time period. The objective was to test the subway's signs ability to convey information. An unobstrusive measure was obtained by having researchers surreptitiously observe the subjects' citywide wanderings. The resulting report was a rich description of frustration and confusion as the subjects experienced it.

Process-oriented. Traditional research methods are largely inadequate for understanding how consumers acquire, organize, and use information in making decisions. The standard methods focus on decision outcomes (who was the purchaser, what was purchased) rather than tapping decision processes. Observational data, however, can be gathered in the form of an extended qualitative pattern, not individual bits and pieces of information. The previous illustration of the mass transit study is a useful example. Instead of having to rely upon self-report data such as "Did you have problems in following the signs?" and "How was the information confusing?", the researcher was able to develop a complete descriptive record of the process that was undertaken by the subject—entrance into the subway, length of time taken to read a sign, asking other passengers, hesitations, wrong moves, acts of frustration, symbols of confidence, and so on. The fact is that people engage in their roles as consumers in logical blocks of activities. They go to the movies or buy season tickets to a concert series or wash the car. It is a natural "stream of behaviors." Unfortunately, we have a tendency to research these activities as subdivided little units, unconnected, with no antecedents and no consequences.

Environmental Context. Consumer behavior does not occur in a vacuum. That is, the decision-making situation is more complex than the direct interaction between consumer(s) and some attitude object. As a simple example, I may have a positive attitude towards hot cocoa, but my behavior (e.g., purchase and use) may be highly dependent upon a situational variable—namely, that it is a cold winter's day. Such variables as physical and social surroundings contribute greatly to the environmental context and lend themselves to observational data. Recently, an electrical manufacturer did a series of observational studies with purchasing agents within a specific industry in order to understand who influenced purchase decisions. The individuals were brought together in a research setting and given the task of choosing several different prototypes of a new product. The manufacturer was not interested in the choice, but in observing and describing the social system which worked to influence the choice process. Such observational data would be important for purposes of fine-tuning industrial advertising and personal selling strategies.

Discovery. Scales, instruments, and questionnaires require that the researcher have prior knowledge of all the key forces in question. While such preconceived brilliance on the part of the researcher may be possible in some situations, in other circumstances researchers should admit their ignorance and take a discovery-oriented approach:

> Some time ago, a well known British ice cream manufacturer was concerned that sales of some of its products in neighborhood shops were not achieving the levels that had been expected from children's enthusiasm for these products as measured through interviews. A direct observation study in neighborhood shops revealed why. The ice cream was kept in top-loading refrigerators, with sides that were so high that many of the children could not see in to pick out the products they wanted. Nor did the young children ask for the product by name. A picture display was devised for the side of the cabinet to enable the children to recognize and so indicate their choice. Sales increased. As with many discoveries, once seen, the solution is very obvious, but it required direct observation in this case to isolate the problem.[30]

As is evident from the example, not only can this approach generate hypotheses or ideas for further inquiry, it can also act as a direct problem-solving method in which solutions are the outcome of a discovery process.

Recall and Guesstimation. As a rule, we neither remember nor predict very well. But, as one set of researchers has pointed out, "All too many research techniques depend entirely on people's retrospective or anticipatory reports of their own behavior."[31] We ask people the likelihood of their purchasing a particular product, and we ask people if they saw an advertisement. And, if Gallup and Harris and Roper have taught us anything, it is that if you ask people a question, they will give you an answer. The alternative offered by observational methods is to record behaviors as they occur. Such qualitative acts do not depend on recall. Instead, the individuals' behaviors are studied as they are happening, enabling researchers to record streams of behavior. This is important because there can be a minimum of congruence between what people say and what people do. Irwin Deutscher, in a book entitled, *What We Say/What We Do* has discussed the evidence. Several of the classic studies include:

> Richard LaPierre in 1934 recorded the treatment that a Chinese couple received in hotels and restaurants. Of the 251 establishments they approached on a trip across the country, only one place refused to accommodate them. Later a questionnaire was sent to each establishment asking "Would you accept members of the Chinese race as guests in your establishment?" Only one positive response was received.

> A small rural community in Kansas was the setting for a 1958 study by Charles Warriner concerning the drinking of alcoholic beverages. Interviews with the citizenry of this "dry" town revealed a consistent personal belief that drinking alcoholic beverages was wrong. However, an unobtrusive garbage search showed that the public expressions of condemnation did not equate to private drinking behavior.

> In 1969, Dannick studied pedestrians crossing at an intersection. Having observed those who crossed against a "Don't Walk" light, he proceeded to question them. A frequent response was that they never engaged in such behavior and, even more frequently, expressed the sentiment that it was an inappropriate thing to do.[32]

Whatever the nature of the observation, it is evident that it is independent of many of the foibles exhibited in verbal responses. When asked, people exaggerate, try to please, try to subvert, try to impress, cheat, and lie. Why not just watch them?

Weaknesses

It is almost more important to be aware of the negative aspects of a particular technique. By concentrating on the advantages, it is relatively easy to become enamored with the method. The result of this one-sidedness, as we have seen, is a researcher who is technique-oriented. In contrast, a problem orientation requires that the technique is chosen on the basis of the problem situation and a review of the strengths and weaknesses of all available solution methods.

Selective Perception. The commonly used saying is "seeing is believing," though of all our senses the eyes are the most easily deceived. Remarkable demonstrations of the unreliability of visual observations are provided by magicians who make lions and tigers disappear, and the street corner huckster who makes his living playing the "shell game." Psychologists have conducted many experiments that have shown that what a person perceives on a particular occasion depends greatly on their state of mind and body at the time, and the "sensitivity" of their sense organs. As Bertrand Russell put it: "There is as yet no way of combining a microscope, a microphone, a thermometer, a galvanometer, etc. into a single organism which will react in an integral manner to the combination of all different stimuli and affect its different sense organs."[33] In our case the camera does lie!

Human perception is highly selective and what people "see" is dependent on their background. Our culture tells us what to see; our childhood socialization instructs us in how to look at the world; and our value systems tell us how to interpret what we see. In other words, what is observed depends on who is looking. If an architect, urban planner, and consumer researcher were to observe the "goings on" at a new hotel, what do you think their findings would indicate? The architect would report on the structural integrity of the building, the urban planner would evalute matters of ingress and egress, and the consumer researcher would describe the clientele. Of course, each of our observers would be correct, though insufficient in their findings, thus confirming the old adage, "We are prone to see what lies behind our eyes rather than what appears before them." Perhaps Goethe said it even better . . . "We see only what we know."

What Is Not Why. The most obvious weakness of observational methods is that they provide information on behavior only, and behavior cannot always be interpreted easily. One episode illustrates this problem.

A man with his arms full of cans throws the armful into a cart at the beginning of the aisle. He pulls the cart by the front along with him down the aisle. He turns around a Rinso Blue box and reads the front for a moment. Then he walks back to the beginning of the aisle and for a moment. Then he walks back to the beginning of the aisle and looks at Oxydol, regular size. He hesitates and picks up a large package of All with the rose bush offer. He leaves this box and walks up the rest of the aisle. He then reads an All box (in a display with the rest of the All's) and puts it back. He backs down the aisle halfway and reads the Dreft box; then further up he reads the Ivory Snow box. He then takes a box of Instant Fels and puts it in the cart.[34]

What was the man looking for? In this case the researchers were able to ask him; his answer: "I am allergic and was looking for one with 'soap' marked on it. I have a terrible reaction to detergents."

Sampling. In a large survey we may be intent on generating conclusions which are generalizable to a population. The sampling, therefore, is done using a probabilistic sampling procedure. However, when using observational techniques, there is a tendency to believe that what is observed is a representative description of a larger population. But the fact remains that the observation is an isolated incident and may be totally unrepresentative of a more general behavior. For example, if we were interested in observing supermarket shopping behavior, as in the previous illustration, it should be realized that behaviors will vary with the kind of store—"It is one thing to shop in a small, crowded, urban market which offers limited selection, and something else again to fill a cart in a large highway store or spacious modern market in suburbia." In addition to differences in shopping environment among stores, behaviors and populations (i.e., husband, wife, children) will vary within the same store at different hours of the day and on different days.

Reactivity. As was previously noted, in some forms of participant observation where the role of the researcher is known to the group under study, the mere presence of the observer means that opinions are made and orientations are developed toward the observer that would not otherwise have occurred. The "typicality" of the event is biased because of this interaction. It is interesting to note that reactivity is not just related to the fact that an observer is present; objectivity can be lost when those being observed are merely aware of their being watched. The classic example of this is the Hawthorne illumination studies which attempted to determine the impact of lighting on productivity. As expected, when better lighting was provided in the experimental group, productivity increased. However, when it was decided that the experiment should be reversed, and the lights dimmed, productivity kept going up. The time came when the workers were practically working by moonlight but productivity was still increasing. The conclusion of the study was that while lighting was probably related to productivity, the more important factor was attention. The simple fact that the workers were being observed was interpreted as their being the center of attention, and they showed their ego-gratification by increasing productivity. Observation influenced behavior. The fact is that all of us have a tendency to "play to the camera."

IMPROVING OBSERVATION

There are a number of general rules for minimizing the disadvantages of observation. This is not to say that the weaknesses can be completely overcome, but the knowledgeable researcher can have a very real impact on the quality of the observational data. For example, in the area of "Reactivity" the researcher has options that would not be available to an interviewer who is conducting focus groups or depth interviews. In these latter techniques, the interviewer/respondent relationship must be personalized. With many observation applications, however, it is not necessary for the observer to be known to the subject. The earlier example of the transit system signage study is an illustration of such nonreactive research. Since the subjects were not aware they were being observed, the unobtrusive measurement could not be biased by any observer/subject interaction. It should also be noted that even when the subject is aware of the presence of an observer or is aware of being under scrutiny, care can be taken to match observer and subject on the basis of age, sex, social class, and so on. The observer becomes a mirror image of the kind of subject being observed. Also, whenever possible, allow for an adjustment period, an initial length of time in which no data are gathered. In a recent study for Kimberly-Clark, a researcher videotaped some 200 hours of diaper changing techniques to assist in a redesign of "Huggies." The researcher noted that "People played to the cameras at first, but it soon became just another part of their daily lives."[35] An illustration is available in the study for the utility company in which cameras were placed in peoples' homes in order to observe the details of thermostat-setting: the researcher made no attempt to gather data until several weeks after the cameras had been installed.

The "Sampling" problem is best handled through a careful examination of the observation situation. In the supermarket example it was noted that shopping behavior varied by type of store, time of day, and other factors. Such insight can be gathered through obvious means of expert judgment (interview store managers or cashiers) and critical thinking (ask yourself what factors could be important). In addition, a series of focus groups or depth interviews could also be used to elicit a listing of potential concerns. When the researcher is satisfied that such factors have been enumerated, efforts can be made to incorporate them into the research design. In this case, the researchers attended to this disadvantage by dividing the total number of observations among time of day, day of week, type of store, *et cetera*.

The problem(s) relating to "Selective Perception" are usually handled through training and multiple observers. Observers should be trained to simply describe, and by using multiple observers we can increase the validity of the findings since the chances are greater that the observers will agree on the "facts."

The "What is Not Why" disadvantage is easily overcome. The researcher must keep "What" separate from "Why." If the objective of the research is merely to describe a situation, then the observational method can stand alone. However, when the problem requires data relating to attitudes, beliefs or motivations, it is necessary for the researcher to add a second stage to the research design. In a study in which the effectiveness of advertisements in comics was analyzed, observation of the children reading the comics quickly revealed that they turned from one feature to the next with barely a glance at the advertisements. An interview stage followed the observations:

> On being questioned about this, they say, 'there is nothing there.' Inserts for coupons are by and large more effective because they require some activity on the part of the child, which thereby increases the child's attention to them.[36]

FINALITIES

Sherlock Holmes

Observation requires an imaginative research design and a developed set of observational skills.

Accurate observation of complex situations is extremely difficult and
observers usually make many errors of which they are not conscious.
Effective observation involves noticing something and giving it significance by relating it to something else noticed or already known;
thus it contains both an element of sense-perception and a mental
element.[37]

The skills do not come without practice, without forcing oneself to observe occurences in minute detail. Every angle should be explored and
every inconsistency revealed. The observer is a chronicler of human behavior with a keen eye and a certain fondness for particulars. Even the
venerable Mr. Watson was forced to admit that Holmesian skills are not
easily developed in the ardent student of observation:

Watson had been watching his companion intently ever since he had
sat down to the breakfast table. Holmes happened to look up and
catch his eye.

"Well, Watson, what are you thinking about?"he asked.

"About you."

"Me?"

"Yes, Holmes, I was thinking how superficial are these tricks of
yours, and how wonderful it is that the public should continue to
show interest in them."

"I quite agree," said Holmes. "In fact, I have a recollection that I
have myself made a similar remark."

"Your methods," said Watson severely, "are really easily acquired."

"No doubt," Holmes answered with a smile. "Perhaps you will yourself give an example of this method of reasoning."

"With pleasure," said Watson. "I am able to say that you were greatly preoccupied when you got up this morning. In addition, you have
a client named Barlow and you have not been successful in his case."

"Excellent!" said Holmes. "You are indeed observant. Any other points?"

"Yes, Holmes. You have put on your black coat, instead of your dressing gown, which proves that you are expecting some important visitor at once. Also, you have taken to financial speculation since you opened the paper, turned to the financial page, and gave a loud exclamation of interest."

"Well, that is very clever of you, Watson. Anything more?"

"I have no doubt that I could find other points, Holmes, but I only give you these few, in order to show you that there are other people in the world who can be as clever as you."

"And some not so clever," said Holmes. "I admit that they are few, but I am afraid, my dear Watson, that I must count you among them."

"What do you mean, Holmes?"

"Well, my dear fellow, I fear your deductions have not been so happy as I should have wished."

"You mean that I was mistaken."

"Just a little that way, I fear. Let us take the points in their order: I did not shave because I have, worse luck, an early meeting with my dentist. His name is Barlow, and the letter was to confirm the appointment. The cricket page is beside the financial one, and I turned to it to find Surrey was holding its own against Kent. But go on, Watson, go on ! It's a very superficial trick, and no doubt you will soon acquire it."[38]

Managerial Insights

Look To Processes. Much of consumer research focuses on isolated incidences. Often we do not fully understand antecedent and consequent conditions, contexts, or situational variables. While it is necessary to focus on specific acts or attitudes, it is important to be able to appreciate the environment in which such events occur. Price sensitivity of movie tickets is one study; going to the movies is another. The attitudes toward the key features of a new bank product is one study; going to the bank is another. Observation methods can provide process information that can encompass many specific consumer behavior activities.

Maintain Anonymity. There are no disciplines that focus on the human condition that do not have a well-developed literature on the negative effect of researcher reactivity. People, when confronted by others, do lie, forget, misinterpret, and exaggerate. Numbers derived from such interactions can be just that—numbers. In some research situations it is of paramount importance to collect data without researcher intrusion. This chapter described the vintage example of Lapiere's study of the treatment of Chinese in hotels and restaurants. In a recent issue of *Business Horizons,* the following commentary was detailed: "A modern-day LaPiere, without the benefit of his observational data and with the benefit of quantitative methods and computer knowledge, could turn out a most enlightening study—perhaps establishing a relationship between attitudes towards Orientals and restaurant seating capacity, geographic location and the number of cars in the parking lot."[39]

Use All Techniques. Though the notion has been examined elsewhere, it deserves repeating: observation methods are the most underutilized techniques in consumer research. Perhaps that is so because they do not sound scientific or perhaps management just won't buy them. But the fact remains that there is a unique kind of understanding that is derived from observation that is simply not possible with any other research methodology. Samuel Johnson once wrote "The use of traveling is to regulate imagination by reality, and instead of thinking how things may be, to see them as they are." Perhaps more consumer researchers should consider getting out from behind their PCs and see things as they happen.

Cases

The following represent a series of case histories in which observation was used as an effective research method:

1. A bank recently instituted a cross-sell program. The nature of this program was to encourage customer service representatives (CSRs) to become something other than just order-takers. When customers inquired about opening a new checking account, the CSR was to actively try to sell them additional services such as IRAs, money market funds, or bank cards. While the success of the program was largely determined by measuring the change in "number of services sold," such a measure could not reveal any problems occurring in the system. In order to generate this kind of data, market researchers went into the branch and opened accounts. They observed the CSRs in their new roles as cross-sell agents. Problems that surfaced were dealt with in a continual finetuning of the cross-sell program.

2. An alternative to traditional drawing or coloring books was developed by a large company. The idea was to have children compose pictures or stories by transferring decals to preprinted background sheets. Four different product configurations were developed and tested on 600 children in play sessions. Management and researchers observed these sessions in order to assess the product concepts in terms of their ease of use, appropriateness of use and level of enjoyment.[40]

3. Shelf arrangement was the topic of one observational study. A large food retailer installed a new slot-type shelf arrangement for canned goods. Although such an arrangement was more cost efficient in comparison to traditional shelf stacking (it took considerably less time to stock the shelves), it was of questionable value to the shopper. A camera was activated when the shopper entering the aisle approached the experimental shelf arrangement (within three feet). Consumer reactions to the slot-type arrangement were compared to the traditional stacking arrangement. Comparisons were made on the basis of time taken to make a choice and relative difficulty in removing the can from the display.

4. A test kitchen was employed by a food manufacturer in order to study the preparation procedures for a new variety of Chinese food. The product, as developed by the manufacturer, consisted of two cans attached together and a package of dry spices. All of this was contained in a larger cardboard package. The manufacturer wanted to test different instructional approaches in order to determine which was easier. Two different versions were tested with researchers imposing differing levels of distractions on

the subjects; some were left alone to prepare the meal, others were engaged in conversation during the test period. Observers (through a one-way mirror) studied the subjects' ability to follow the steps described on the package, particularly noting the amount of elapsed time, fumbling with package, and instructional errors.

ENDNOTES

[1]Alsop, Ronald (1986), "People Watchers Seek Clues to Consumers' True Behavior," *The Wall Street Journal,* (September 4), p. 29.

[2]Ardrey, Robert (1961), *African Genesis* in Webb, Eugene et al., p. 152.

[3]Feshbach, S. and N. Feshbach (1983), "Influence of the Stimulus Object Upon the Complementary and Supplementary Projection of Fear," *Journal of Abnormal and Social Psychology,* 66, p. 499.

[4]Webb, Eugene J. et al., (1966), *Unobtrusive Measures,* (Rand McNally: Chicago).

[5]Hicks, J. W. and R. L. Kohls (1955), "Memotion Study as a Method of Measuring Consumer Behavior," *The Journal of Marketing*, October, p. 168.

[6]Reid, Leonard N. (1979), "The Impact of Family Group Interaction on Children's Understanding of Television Advertising," *Journal of Advertising Research,* 8, Summer, pp. 13-19.

[7]Barker and Wright (1951), *One Boy's Day.*

[8]Tull, Donald S. and Del I. Hawkins (1980), *Marketing Research,* (Macmillan: New York), p. 325.

[9]Seymour, Daniel T. (1981), unpublished dissertation.

[10]Churchill, Gilbert (1983), *Marketing Research*, (The Dryden Press: New York), p. 252.

[11]Klein, Frederick C. (1983), "Researcher Probes Consumers Using Anthropological Skills," *The Wall Street Journal,* July 7, p. 25.

[12]Venkatesan, M. (1966), "Experimental Study of Consumer Behavior Conformity and Independences," *Journal of Marketing Research,* Nov., pp. 384–7.

[13]Richer, John (1981), "Observation, Ethology, and Marketing Research," *European Research,* 9, January, p.23.

[14]Harrison, Michael (1972), *In the Footsteps of Sherlock Holmes* (Drake Publishing Co.: New York), p. 218.

[15]Sawyer, H. G. (1961), "The Meaning of Numbers," Speech before the American Association of Advertising Agencies.

[16]"In Tuscon, Students are Down in Dumps, But Most are Happy," *The Wall Street Journal,* December 5, 1975, pp. 1–25.

[17]Rathje, W. J., W.W. Hughes and S. L. Jernigon (1976), "The Science of Garbage: Following the Consumer Through His Garbage Can," in W. Locander (ed.), *Business Proceedings* (American Marketing Association), pp. 56-64.

[18]Alsop, Ronald (1986), "'People Watchers' Seek Clues to Consumers' True Behavior," *The Wall Street Journal,* September 4, p.29.

[19]Richer, op. cit.

[20]Whyte, William (1955), *Street Corner Society,* (University of Chicago Press: Chicago).

[21]Douglas, Susan P., C. Samuel Craig and Jean-Philippe Faivre (1981), "Protocols in Consumer Research," *Research in Marketing,* J. Sheth (ed.), (JAI Press: Greenwich, CT), p.33.

[22]King, Robert H. (1969), "A Study of the Problem of Building a Model to Stimulate the Cognitive Processes of a Shopper in a Supermarket," in

George H. Haines (ed.), Co*nsumer Behavior: Learning Models of Purchasing,* (The Free Press: New York), pp. 22–67.

[23]Discussed in Boehm, Ann E. and Richard Weinberg (1977), *The Classroom Observer,* (Teachers College Press: New York), p. 49.

[24]Douglas, Craig et al., op. cit., p. 33.

[25]Seymour, op. cit.

[26]Arndt, Johan and Crane, Edgar (1975), "Marital Roles in Intrafamilial Decision Making on Spending Matters," *American Marketing Association Proceedings,* Ronald Curhan (ed.), (American Marketing Association: Chicago), pp. 63–6.

[27]Bales, Robert F. (1950), *Interaction Process Analysis,* (Reading, MA: Addison-Wesley).

[28]McGrew, W. C., (1972), *An Ethological Study of Children's Behavior,* (Academic Press: New York), p. 25.

[29]Rathje, et al., op. cit.

[30]Richer, op. cit.

[31]Selltiz, Claire et al. (1966), *Research Methods in Social Relations,* (Holt, Rinehart, and Winston: New York), p. 201.

[32]Deutscher, Irwin (1973), *What We Say/What We Do,* (Scott Foresman: Glenview, IL).

[33]Russell, Bertrand (1927), *An Outline of Philosophy,* p. 63.

[34]Wells, William D. and Leonard A. Lo Sciuto (1966), "Direct Observation of Purchasing Behavior," *Journal of Marketing Research*, August, p. 228.

[35]Alsop, op. cit.

[36]Richer, op cit.

[37]Beveridge, op. cit.

[38]Doyle, Sir Arthur Conan, *How Watson Learned the Trick in Sherlock Holmes*, Jack Tracy (ed.), (Boston: Houghton Mifflin).

[39]Seymour, Daniel T. (1984), "Numbers Don't Lie—Do They?," *Business Horizons,* 27 (November/December), p. 37.

[40]Tull, Donald S. and Del I. Hawkins (1980), *Marketing Research*, (Macmillan: New York), p. 1.

CHAPTER FOUR

GROUP INTERVIEWING

Many information users (managers) and a number of information generators (researchers) see the group interview (focus group) and qualitative research as being equivalent. For those of us who are firm believers in the advantages of qualitative research, the fact that a qualitative technique is being used is heartening. And it is being used.

After 25 years of pursuing affluent, frequent-traveling businessmen, American Express has won over about 40% of those it considers worthy of its card. Success had been fueled, in past years, by the "Do You Know Me?" advertising campaign which has defined prestige as success and attainment by using such individuals as Benny Goodman, Jesse Owens, George Gallup and Sam Ervin. More recent research, however, showed that the sort of prestige promoted in the "Do You Know Me?" ads appealed mostly to men. In fact, American Express estimates that its 2.5 million female cardholders represent only about 20 percent of the women that meet its financial, occupational and life-style criteria (male cardholders outnumber women 4 to 1). The reasons why became clearer early last year when American Express executives listened to groups of women, participants in focus-group interviews, discuss credit cards. "What absolutely floored me," recalled Jerry Welsh, senior vice president, "was the irony that they were so familiar with American Express and laudatory about it, yet they didn't see the American Express card as something for them." The new "Interesting Lives" campaign defines prestige as leading an interesting, varied, unexpectedly rich life. In one TV ad, a briefcase-toting woman takes her husband to dinner to celebrate her first American Express card. In another, a mother—her marital status undisclosed—trades wise cracks with her kids in a restaurant. And a print ad features a dress-for-success woman leaving a sporting goods shop, carrying her briefcase in one hand and a lacrosse stick in the other.[1]

Such examples as the American Express research are not uncommon. The American Marketing Association and Marketing Science Institute found that 51 percent of 433 research managers and 62 percent of research suppliers frequently used focus groups in conducting research. Only demographic and usage segmentation techniques were more often used by these managers and suppliers.[2] But the focus-group technique, just as all other techniques, is not appropriate for all situations. It has many unique advantages but it also has numerous disadvantages. It is only by having a thorough knowledge of the method that a researcher can make an informed decision to use a focus-group, another qualitative approach, or, instead, to "generate some numbers."

The current faddish popularity of focus groups is largely due to the characteristics of the technique: they are quick, easy, and the resulting data are appealing to management. As such, the strengths of the focus- group technique combine to create a significant weakness. That is, the choice to use the technique is based upon only these appealing characteristics, instead of analyzing the problem situation and weighing the advantages and disadvantages of all available techniques. It is almost too easy to "do some groups." Matthew Miles has attached a label to the kind of research which follows this thinking—the "attractive nuisance":

> The legal doctrine of an "attractive nuisance" is simply illustrated by what happens if you abandon a car in your backyard: if neighboring children come eagerly to play in it, you are liable for their injuries.[3]

In addition to the inherent attractiveness of the focus-group technique, its popularity is also due to its lack of structure. In fact, this lack of structure is evident when attempting to find a definition of "focus-group interviewing." Occasionally, some hardy soul makes an attempt to do so as an introduction to an article or book chapter. In such instances, however, the definition is usually limited to a small set of criteria; for example, a focus group is " . . . a number of interacting individuals having a community of interests."[4] Given such elusiveness, it can also be conjectured that the popularity of this technique has almost as much to do with "what it is not", as "what it is." As noted in a recent Advertising Research Foundation (1985) publication, it is not burdened with a definitive list of specific standards:

> As qualitative research has evolved, the focus-group interview has gained share among qualitative techniques, largely because this particular form of qualitative research has proved so adaptable to so many different kinds of research questions. Indeed it is possible that the focus-group format is in some sense *too* adaptable—so adaptable

that it gets employed semi-automatically when some other less-familiar technique would be more informative or more efficient.[5]

A broad spectrum of opinions about focus groups exists among marketing and advertising researchers. The following quotes from respected scholars and practitioners exemplify the current state of affairs. Everyone has an opinion:

A senior account executive emerged from the viewing room in a kind of state of shock after a focus-group session. He was an excellent and dedicated account man. I know because I worked with him on one of my earliest projects, even when qualitative research was relatively unfamiliar. He had made every effort to do a good job for his client and for his consumer. Yet, on this occasion, he said, "For 20 years I've been on this brand and I must say that this is the first time I can feel that I really understand the consumer."[6]

Probably no market research methodology is employed as regularly by practitioners with as little understanding as focus groups. Like putty, the technique seems to be readily adaptable to whatever research problem is extant.[7]

A well-known market researcher claims that, "in most cases, focus groups should be priced out as client entertainment rather than research."[8]

I remember a client sitting next to me at one of these meetings who left the room saying, "If I ever considered using focus groups, this would certainly convince me to forget it. What they're trying to tell me is that 'anything goes' and that can't be the way it is."[9]

And finally, to put everything into a confusing tailspin, one of our most respected colleagues has written in a chapter on "Group Interviewing" the following under a section entitled "How Can Anything So Bad Be Good?":

Group interviewing violates most of the accepted canons of survey research. Samples are invariably small and never selected by probability methods. Questions are not asked the same way each time.

Responses are not independent. Some respondents inflict their opinions on others; some contribute little or nothing at all. Results are difficult or impossible to quantify and are not grist for the statistical mill. Conclusions depend on the analyst's interpretive skill. The investigator can easily influence the results. With these glaring defects, why have group interviews been so widely used?[10]

Perhaps we need to return to the notion of the "levels of meaning" discussed in Chapter One to give a more intellectually satisfying reason for the popularity of focus groups. As we cut through the layers of meaning that humans attach to objects and events, we move from spontaneous, public realities to unconscious, private thoughts. Structured questionnaires, the life-blood of consumer researchers, are quite appropriate for measuring the conscious factors related to consumption. Experimentation can establish associations and observation methods can describe the nature of purchase patterns. As the level of the decision process being studied becomes more private (e.g. rationalization and explanation), the level of the investigatory tools must adapt.

The focus-group interview, or group depth interview, is a technique that had its genesis in psychological group therapy. The concept is based on the assumption that individuals who share a problem will be more willing to discuss it within the security of others sharing the same problem. The group aspect, therefore, consists of a number of interacting individuals having a community of interests. The interaction is the result of the group setting causing the opinions of each person to be considered by the others. In contrast to the individual interview in which the flow of information is unidirectional, the group provides an information network which enables individuals to submit ideas as well as respond to the ideas of others. Group cohesiveness results from individuals identifying with other individuals or sharing a common interest, whether it is the topic of alcoholism, manic depression, a new TV sitcom pilot or an advertising concept.

As consumer needs became the target of product and service marketers, it was inevitable that additional information was required to describe the various market segments. The greater need to know has quickly pushed beyond the level of conscious factors. Demographic segmentation and usage patterns are insufficient descriptions. Group interviewing has been seen to be the mechanism for generating "rationalization and explanation" data useful in understanding consumer behavior. The American Express example is an appropriate illustration of the ability of the group interview to explain a specific behavior.

In place of a rigid set of standards, the focus-group method has evolved around a loose collection of practices that relate to the practical decisions which must be made when setting up and conducting group interviewing. The following section of this chapter will describe and discuss those major decisions.

RESEARCH DESIGN DECISIONS

The technique is, supposedly, unencumbered by "set-in-concrete" rules, but many articles take just the opposite stance. Such normative statements as "The ideal focus group has between 8 and 10 members" or "serving alcoholic beverages turns the session into a carnival atmosphere" detract from the flexibility inherent in the technique. At times, mini-groups of 4 to 5 people appear to work exceptionally well and serving Diet-Coke to a focus group of long-haul truckers may constitute a slight misjudgment of lifestyle. This section, then, will not be on a laundry list of "do's and don'ts", but rather a discussion of important design issues.

Choosing a Moderator

The consensus seems to be that the moderator is *the* essential component present in all successful focus-group interviews: "The one thing on which everyone agrees with respect to focus-group interviews is that the moderator's role is of prime importance to success."[11] The major reason for this fact is that the moderator plays field general and must adopt a specific role (which changes depending on the topic, the facilities, the group members, *et cetera*). For example, the moderator can function at any place along a "role continuum" from directive to nondirective. The directive approach means that the moderator maintains control of the discussion, does most of the questioning and sticks to the specific topics of the moderator guide. At the nondirective extreme the moderator sets the initial topic of discussion and then only interjects when the discussion wanders too far afield. It is obvious, then, that the moderator is the catalyst and even when he or she is not speaking, it is for a purpose—to encourage spontaneity in a nonevaluative, nonthreatening environment.

Several moderator characteristics appear to be particularly important to the quality of the resulting data. First, one of the main advantages of the focus-group technique is the benefits which accrue from the social interaction among group members. The group effect can be exciting and emotionally provocative. But it should also be noted that the group can have a number of negative characteristics. It is, therefore, of utmost importance that a moderator has the ability to use group dynamics skillfully in order to deal with ". . . a quiet, passive group, an overly exuberant group, an outspoken group member who is unqualified, a group which consistently goes off on a tangent, a group which appears to be giving inconsistent responses, a group which does not understand the question, a group which misses the point completely, a group which is inarticulate, a hostile group or group member, a nervous, tense group discussing a sensitive subject, *et cetera.".*[12]

A second extremely important moderator characteristic is the ability to listen. Being a good listener may be something of a lost art in modern society. Everyone wants to be heard but few people make a conscious effort to actually do any hearing; and yet that it is the key to knowledge. Or as the proverb goes: "He that speaks, sows; he that hears, reaps." A focus-group moderator is part psychoanalyst. He or she must question, probe, explore, retreat, cajole, flatter, punish, control and entice but above all else be sincerely empathic—really care about what others have to say and try to identify with them. Such empathy is based on the ability to listen.

There are two different types of flexibility which are crucial traits in a focus-group moderator: planned and unplanned. The first variety is directly related to a moderator having done his homework and then, accordingly, adjusting his or her appearance, approach and style. Moderators should not develop a standardized method to conducting focus-groups. The ideal moderator, instead, should be able to adopt a chameleon-like approach to each focus-group session. For example, a group done with brides-to-be should be totally different from a group in which industrial purchasing agents are the members. Virtually everything from the moderator's clothing to the room arrangement may change. There are even some moderators who have the ability to subtly change their accent and mannerisms to reflect the geographic region in which the group is being held.

A second (unplanned) type of flexibility is necessary to be an effective moderator. Even in the most directive groups where the moderator closely follows the moderator guide, the session is a lot more than just going in and asking the questions—discussion guides are not questionnaires! Every session has the potential for disaster and, consequently, every moderator should have the boxer's skill of quick feet and the talent of a politician for changing course in mid-stream:

> The group interview should be conducted the way one walks across a rope bridge. The handrails are gripped firmly and the objective is kept in mind constantly. If the bottom foot rope should break, the walk is continued hand over hand until the destination is reached. This requires an ability to improvise and alter predetermined plans amid the distractions of the group process.[13]

In addition to these major characteristics, the successful moderator should also have a series of less obvious personal traits that are indicative of their ability to get close to people. One practitioner has noted several additional attributes:

Are Animated And Spontaneous. Someone with a dull personality will not be able to control focus groups. Spontaneity is vital for a moderator to take advantage of the great many stimuli during a session.

Have A Sense Of Humor. I don't mean telling canned jokes but finding latent humor possibilities in ordinary situations. This quality, more important than it may seem, is strongly related to imagination, creativity, and spontaneity, all needed in qualitative research.

Are Sensitive. The moderator is constantly aware of the mood and the demeanor of the participants and knows that the strongest "clues" in "reading" the group will come from what is happening and from the emotional affect he perceives in the respondents. He is always listening with a particularly keen "third" ear.

Admit Their Own Biases. Complete objectivity is impossible, but we can aim for recognition of our own personal feelings towards the subject with which we're dealing. If qualitative researchers talk about their own experiences or feelings related to a project, a client doesn't necessarily have to get nervous about their objectivity. The key point is whether we can be honest and introspective enough to understand these biases and professionally detach ourselves from them in our work.

Express Thoughts Clearly. The moderator must frame questions quickly, and, if these cannot be stated simply, the session will not succeed.[14]

Finally, it must be mentioned that watching a topnotch focus-group moderator at work is much akin to watching an athlete run the Boston Marathon. His easy motion, his effortless grace gives you the feeling that you could do that as well. Most people, however, have the sense to touch base with reality long enough to not bother sending in their entrance fee for the next marathon. Unfortunately, such is not the case with moderating focus groups. There are, arguably, only a handful of thoroughly knowledgeable and professional moderators in the country. A second tier contains a goodly number of moderators who are adequate for most tasks. After that, however, the level of competency falls off rapidly, with many persons who have mastered Psychology 201 considering themselves prepared for moderating.

Recruiting a Group

The moderator's skills are of little consequence if they find themselves faced with a roomful of unqualified respondents who have no experience or background in the category from which to draw. While a considerable amount of time can be spent defining the management problem, listening to focus groups and trying to relate the data to decision making, many researchers neglect to devote a requisite amount of time to recruiting practices. Several areas of recruiting are crucial and require active involvement.

First, the desired composition of the groups must be defined. In many situations this necessitates a discussion session between the client (or information user), the researcher, and a field or recruiting service. Since the recruiting function is often done with an outside field service, your responsibility in working with recruiters is to tell them *exactly* who you want, and just as importantly, who you don't want in your groups. Key issues relative to recruiting the appropriate group composition include the following:

Mix. Usually it is a good practice to try to develop a homogeneous cast of group members, especially as regards social class, stage in life cycle, and sex. When social classes are mixed, the more literate and articulate members tend to dominate. Members of different life-cycle stages can have too varied needs, problems, resources, experiences and perceptions. Sex differences can be problematic when dealing with sensitive or personal issues. This is not to say, however, that heterogeneity is not important in some situations. For example, when the objective of a session is idea generation, wider diversity of backgrounds is necessary. At other times, in order to explore the rationale for product adoption, the mix may call for a split of users and nonusers.

Time. While one of the major strengths of focus-group research is that groups can be done faster than most alternative forms of research, problem can arise from emergency recruiting. When crisis recruiting is done, as it often is, there is a tendency to sacrifice the ideal composition of the group for warm bodies. Relatives and secretaries in the recruiting service end up in emergency groups. Or your requested group of housewives between the ages of 35 - 50 years old are, coincidentally, all wives of Boston policemen—hardly a diverse set of attitudes.

Virgins. Everyone wants virgin respondents who have never participated in a group discussion before. From the recruiter's point of view, it is much less expensive to generate willing members from a pool of people who have been involved in previous groups. The "professional" group member begins to see group participation as a sort of game in which if they give the right answers they get to come back again. Many have heard the anecdote of the nine housewives from Brooklyn who do all the group sessions for New York-based companies. Introductions may begin with "Oh, didn't know you were in this one, Ethel. Haven't seen you since 'shampoos' last Thursday."

Everyone involved with focus-group research should also be aware of the methods by which group members are selected. In many situations, groups are of a very defined nature—doctors, dancers, scuba divers, purchasing agents, and so on. In such cases the telephone book, referrals, association membership lists, or sales receipts represent easy ways to recruit a group. If the group is not as uniquely homogeneous as this, other recruiting methods can be used. The basic ones are:

Random Recruiting—Telephone interviewing on a random-digit-dialing basis (most expensive).

Data-Bank Recruiting—Data bank contains demographic information of individuals who have expressed a prior willingness to participate (economical and efficient because refusals decrease).

Intercept Recruiting—Shopping malls are used to confront shoppers.

Organization Recruiting—Access to the membership list of an organization (usually for a donation).

Supplied-List Recruiting—The client can supply a list of their own customers.

Third-Party Recruiting—Having a recruited group member refer another person.

Each of these methods has advantages and disadvantages that the researcher should explore. For example, organization recruiting may be less expensive and more convenient but the fact remains that members of the Phoenix German-American Club or the Young Republicans can have a very similar, and restricted, view of the world.

The operational side of the recruiting comes in the "How?" stage. Having decided who we will recruit and where we will get them, we must finally decide on the specifics of a screener for selection purposes. The screener is the device that translates the qualification criteria into questions, which by their answers, will either render a respondent acceptable or unacceptable. The three major areas of questioning are:

1. Demographics: Questions that limit the group by age, income, education, etc. For example, "Do you have teenage children?"
2. Incidence: The degree or level of occurrence related to use of a product or service. For example, "Are you a registered voter?" or "Have you used a floor wax in the previous month?"
3. Participation: The number of times the individual has participated in a focus-group session. The usual question, unless virgin members are requested, is "Have you participated in a focus group in the last six months?"

The Size of a Group

There has certainly been no lack of opinion on this topic. Everyone has a ideal number in mind based upon what they have seen work, and not work, for them. The most common response to the question "How many in a group?" is 8 to 12. Smith[15], Calder[16], and Bellenger et. al[17] seem to agree that the ideal group size is between 8 and 12 given that "fewer than 8 is likely to burden eash individual, while more than 12 tends to reduce each member's participation."[18] Some practitioners believe the number can go as low as 5[19]; others see as many as 20 being a viable number.[20] Still others get very hard-headed about the issue, "I am going to be very dogmatic on this point and say that no group discussion should ever have more than eight respondents."[21]

Let me add another voice to the din by saying that there is no single correct size for a group. The range of 5 to 20 is acceptable since the lower limit of the group is necessary by the fact that a critical mass is required for an aggregation of individuals to become an interacting group.[22] An upper limit is required because of the inability of each person to comment adequately and interact during an acceptable time frame. But the specifics of group size should be determined by a number of relevant factors: (1) the physical limitations of the interview area, (2) the personal style and preference of the moderator, (3) the types of group participants, (4) the subject matter, (5) the number of groups being done, (6) the length of the interview guide, (7) the budget for the project, and the (8) nature of the management problem. For example, Fern in a empirical study found that eight-member groups generated significantly more ideas than four-member groups.[23] Larger numbers, therefore, seem to be best when the research objective entails brainstorming and idea generation. In contrast, the use of mini-groups (4 or 5 people) lasting 45 minutes are good for structured situations such as package testing. They are also helpful for interviewing professionals like doctors and lawyers who tend to have well developed opinions, and almost imperative for children, so that the moderator can maintain control.[24]

The Number of Groups

When involved with quantitative procedures and probability sampling it is necessary to have measures of the error that can be allowed, a level of confidence, and an estimate of the standard deviation of the population. The different numbers are then plugged into the appropriate formula and out comes the sample size. With nonprobability samples, however, the issue of sample size is not so well defined. There would seem to be at least three different issues that may effect the researcher's decision on the number of groups to conduct.

1. Market segments: Regional differences or groupings by age, sex, social class, user/nonuser may require two or three sessions within each grouping.

2. Time and cost: In some situations the driving force behind the decision is a lack of time or lack of funds to pay for additional groups.

3. Marginal utility: The first interview in an unfamiliar area yields a great deal of new information. The second yields less and as more interviews occur it becomes obvious that little new information is to be gained from doing "one more group."

A main problem arises when researchers attempt to apply "quantitative thinking" to a qualitative technique by increasing the number of groups in order to estimate a population attitude. This thinking is inappropriate for several reasons. First, the cost of conducting enough groups to reach a minimum number of respondents for statistical estimation purposes would be prohibitively expensive. And second, even if the financial cost could be absorbed, the sampling procedure would still be of a nonprobability variety, as recently noted by one practitioner:

Group discussions are useful tools for qualitative research, but they fail to satisfy most of the demands of a quantitative study. First, groups are not large-scale research studies. Four group discussions would include fewer than 50 individuals; a random quantitative survey of only 50 would have a sampling variation of up to plus-or-minus 14 percent, probably too large for any meaningful conclusions. Second, group discussions are not based on random selection. Group participants are people who are available on the night of a discussion, willing (and able) to get to a discussion facility, and (often) easily reachable, either through a group facility's data back, or because they happened to be wandering in the right shopping mall. In addition, once qualified individuals are identified for a discussion, generally fewer than one in four will be willing to attend, and then only when they are paid $25–$150.[25]

The Location and Physical Environment

Group interviews can be conducted in a number of locations; in respondents' homes, in a client's office building, or in a neutral setting (supplier's facilities, hotel meeting rooms, and such). Of course, each of these different locations offers some advantages and disadvantages that impact the final decision. The private home, for example, offers a friendly, warm atmosphere which may be conducive to lowering inhibitions. But the disadvantages include the fact that the location is usually not well-known to other participants and directions become a problem. Also, the spatial arrangements may not be conducive to interaction and the informal atmosphere may lead to inattentiveness on the part of the group members: " . . . in such a setting there is a lot of fumbling with clipboards, pencils, coffee cups and ashtrays."[26] It should also be noted that there is the ever-present problem of interruptions:

> At least once during an in-home interview the doorbell (or telephone) will ring. The hostess will leap up, trip over the microphone cord, rush to the door, and conduct a breathless conversation in tones loud enough to disrupt the interview but soft enough to ensure its continuation.[27]

The second location option is to hold the group meeting in the client's office building. While this strongly increases the probability of the client attending and allows client-related equipment to be used (e.g. projectors, samples, prototypes), the group members can start acting like corporate consultants. In the mahogany-conference-table setting, many respondents forget their role as consumers and magically transform themselves into experts. And finally, it is obvious that with such a location the client foregoes any anonymity. All of the biases that may be related to the client's identity become manifest.

A neutral location has one major disadvantage—it will cost you something and can be very expensive. But for this expense you usually receive a professional set-up that overcomes many of the previous disadvantages. Most locations are in central areas with easy directions, the rooms are designed with one-way mirrors and recording devices; and you can be reasonably assured of no inopportune doorbell ringing. Also suppliers often have more than one room with different arrangements. One room may appear to be a modest, "lived-in" looking living room with couches and chairs. Such a room would be more appropriate for housewives or couples discussing various consumer-related problems. Another room may be more formal with a conference table and straight-back chairs. This setting is more appropriate for groups consisting of business and professional people, or for studying advertising concepts, handling prototypes, or engaging in paper and pencil tasks.

Once the choice of a location has been made a second set of decisions must be made concerning the physical environment established at any given site. The physical surroundings are a situational influence which can alter the nature of the interaction among group members. For example, the four sensory perceptions can be extremely influential: (1) visual perceptions—color, brightness, size, shapes; (2) aural perceptions—volume, pitch; (3) olfactory perceptions—scent, freshness; and (4) tactile perceptions—softness, smoothness, temperature. These sensory influences can be manipulated to create an appropriate atmosphere. In addition to these sensory inputs, the physical relationship of the seating arrangement will also influence the group. The following four arrangements will result in different kinds of social interactions, power relationships, and degree of formality:

Random/Living Room. This arrangement is the most informal and may help inhibited people feel more comfortable. Some people, however, will be able to remove themselves physically from the conversation by sinking into a couch or hiding in a corner. It is difficult for the moderator to exert all of his or her influence when the locus of communication is elsewhere; hence an extremely non-directive arrangement.

Circular/Conference. Such an arrangement promotes the maximum amount of social interaction. The moderator has a lower level of power because the configuration relegates the moderator to an equal position among the other members.

Rectangular/Conference. The locus of communication is on the moderator and, as such, s/he has increased power. The arrangement is historically formal and the moderator is in the position to direct proceedings.

Elliptical/Conference. This is the most directive configuration since the members are physically turned toward the moderator. The locus of communication is centered on the moderator but there is also a good deal of member interaction in the same manner as a circular/conference setting.

Adding Equipment

There is a vast array of additional equipment that one might consider when conducting a group session. Such devices as overhead projectors, movie projectors, flip charts, props, and prototypes are legitimate; the rule being "Whatever you need to get the point across, use!" Several more elaborate methods, however, are not quite so straightforward. The most obvious of these methods is the process of audio taping the session. Virtually all group interviews are now being audio taped; some are later transcribed for ease of analysis. While the advantages to such taping are apparent, there are several minor concerns. Anonymity has traditionally been an issue but in current times it is only on very rare occasions that a respondent objects to the procedure. The moderator, nonetheless, should point out that the session is being taped and the microphone should be placed in an unobtrusive position. A second problem is the difficulty involved in trying to decipher taped discussions in which several members talk at the same time. The more non-directive the setting, the greater the tendency for such side conversations to become troublesome. It is usually worthwhile for the moderator to begin a session with a short comment concerning the fact that the session is being taped and, consequently, it is important that "only one person speak at a time."

Videotaping is occuring with greater frequency, although the value of the exercise is questionable. Obviously, the equipment and a professional cameraman are expensive. Also, manipulating the seating arrangments and lighting are bothersome details which may detract from the session. An interesting perspective is offered by one moderator:

...I have found as this group interviewing business becomes more elaborate, clients are requesting videotaping more frequently. My guess is that in many of these cases the videotapes end up being stored on a shelf and are never looked at again. Few people have the interest or stamina to sit and stare at eight or ten hours of film after the fact, so if the tape is going to be used at all it should be edited. This is an extremely time-consuming process, and no one can have an appreciation of how much time it takes until he has been through it once. And believe me, once is enough. Both the filming and the editing are expensive, and my feeling is that much of the time and money spent on videotape might have been better invested else-where.[28]

It should be noted, however, that videotaping should be seriously considered in at least two situations. First, it can be extremely useful when physical activity is important to the study: children playing with toys or opening boxes; adults who are required to use their hands or undertake activites such as eating, drinking, cooking, assembling something, or handling a prototype. Second, videotaping is required if the researcher is considering coding various behaviors but is reluctant to specify what those behaviors are prior to the group sessions. As was explained in the previous chapter on Observation Methods, "post-coding" entails the review of behaviors after they have occured. A series of categories may be extracted from viewing a video tape and used for analyzing future behaviors.

A more controversial piece of equipment is the one-way mirror. When a mirror is available it enables the client(s) to observe the proceedings without inhibiting the group's spontaneity and interaction by their physical presence. It is a means to enable a decision maker to get close to the people. Again, it is imperative that group members be informed of the existence of the mirror and of the fact that people are viewing their activities.

The general disadvantage of cameras, video equipment and mirrors is that they all reinforce the "artificiality" of the situation. They can create a carnival-like atmosphere in which the group members play roles—smart, cute, nonchalant, angry. Everday, common consumers can become experts as they perform in the "theatre of research."

Finally, there are a large number of technological innovations that have been used for special situations. While many research consulting operations have, undoubtedly, used such innovations to differentiate themselves from other suppliers, the following "use groupings " may have some limited, practical application:

Consumption Processes. Video TAT (Thematic Apperception Test) is a video of a consumption process (drying hair, operating an automatic teller machine, *et cetera.*). Group members are shown the entire sequence in order to get a feel for the complete process. Then, during a second showing, the tape is stopped at various points and the respondents asked to react to the event. Because it recreates the process, the video TAT minimizes the distortion of past events and sets a uniform context.[29]

Dispersed Members. A second innovation is the use of teleconferencing for conducting group interviews. While there are a number of drawbacks, in some situations it may be the only way of eliciting group-interactive data from individuals who are geographically dispersed.

Computer-Assisted Choices. In order to systematize data collection, it is possible to use a computer-assisted system to enable consumers to do paired attribute comparisons.[30] Another computer-assisted device has been used to input directly participants' reactions to visual and auditory test material. Having anonymously recorded their reactions, the members are then asked to discuss their responses.[31]

Guiding the Moderator

The moderator's guide is the main vehicle by which the management problem is translated into a research problem in the form of a series of questions or statements. It is an outline which ensures the moderator that all the topics will be covered and, as such, functions as a checklist. While most guides differ extensively by topic, some researchers impose a standardized format on the material. For example, Lautman uses an information requirement framework as the basis for a system for developing comprehensive moderator guides.[32] The following represents a sampling of topic areas and questions concerning a cookware example:

Definition of significant classes of the attitude object:
"What kinds of cookware are there?"

Brand awareness:
"Which brands of cookware are you familiar with?"

Evaluation of attitude objects:
"Which brand is best, worst, and why?"

Situational context/relevant others:
"How, when and where do you use cookware?

Attributes of the attitude object for each situational context:
Physical attributes—"When you think about cooking with aluminum pans, what features of the cookware come to mind?"

Interpersonal—"Does anyone in your family care what type of cookware you use?"

Affective—"Do you have any special feelings towards particular pots and pans?"

In addition to providing a checklist of topics, the moderator's guide should also function as an organization of materials, thereby promoting a logical approach to the problem under investigation:

> For example, if you are doing some research on a new hot breakfast cereal, you might want to begin with a discussion of what is served at breakfast and then refine that by having respondents describe weekday versus weekend breakfasts. From there you might move on to focus on cereals, both hot and cold, then narrow down to hot cereals only. At this point you would probably introduce the concept for the new product, and you might even have some actual product prepared for respondents to taste. Just like a good story, a group discussion should have a beginning, a middle, and an end.[33]

Typically, as in this example, the movement is from the general to the specific. Such a progression allows the moderator to gain a better understanding of the consumer's framework for making decisions.

The length of the moderator's guide can vary from one page to four or five. The average is probably two or three typed, double-spaced pages.

Factors that determine the length include the duration of the session, the topic matter, and the style of the moderator. For example, the following illustration is a one-page moderator's guide for a group session on travelers checks:

Moderator Introduction: Moderator will introduce himself, say a few words about the purpose of the research and explain procedures.

Respondent Introduction: Each respondent will be asked to state his/her first name, place of residence and occupation.

• General discussion of travelers checks.

• Situations in which to use travelers checks.

• Situations in which not to use travelers checks.

• Respondents complete self-administered questionnaire "A" on awareness.

• Discussion.
• Similarities/differences among various travelers checks.

• Where/why/how obtained travelers checks presently used.

• Selectivity (do you request - have choice - just accept what is offered, or just what?).

• Perceived cost of travelers checks currently used.

• Respondents complete self-administered questionnaire "B" on selection.

• Discussion.

• Specific probes on various travelers checks presently being offered: (what if _____ offered would you accept/refuse or just what?):

American Express Travelers Checks
Master Card Travelers Checks
Visa Travelers Checks
Bank of America Travelers Checks
Thomas Cook Travelers Checks
CitiCorp Travelers Checks
Barclay's Travelers Checks

• "Horror" stories/good experiences.

• Wrap up.

Several important points need to be made as to what a moderator's guide is not. First, the guide is not an ironclad contract with the client. As one researcher recently described it: "Guides are not questionnaires; there is no need to be as precise with phraseology as there is with a questionnaire where consistent questions are to be administered by many different interviewers."[34] It must be seen as the best possible outline that the researcher can design; and in most situations, if the proper amount of time has been devoted to it, the guide works out quite well. At times, however, disaster strikes (usually with the first session in an untested area). At such a point, the moderator must fall back on his or her "flexibility" attribute and extemporize. It is extremely frustrating to watch a group take off in a very fruitful but unforeseen direction and have the moderator cut the conversation short in order to stick to the guide. In such situations the moderator becomes merely a "question-asker" and nothing more. The feedback from the group members should be first and foremost—probing, coaxing, and reacting to each person's comments. When the moderator is too busy looking at the guide to listen, the quality of the interaction will be minimal.

CONDUCTING THE GROUP

The topics that have been discussed so far are important because they encompass many of the pre-group details. The glamourous part comes when the respondents begin to arrive for a group session. Then it becomes a challenge, a rewarding, exciting process of mental give-and- take. But it is important to remember that the glamour part can be an expensive waste of time and money if the requisite amount of homework has not been done.

Getting Started

The initial part of each session should be devoted to an introduction. The objective of this task is to familiarize everyone with everyone else and to "loosen up" the group. Most people (it is to be hoped) have not previously attended a group interviewing session and, consequently, they may be anxious as to the procedure and expectations. All members can be asked to give their names, where they live and their occupations. This familiarization stage should also be used to set the tone for the group. For example, the moderator can could refer to everyone by their first name and say "Bristol is a beautiful little town—you must be close to the water." Or perhaps "You mentioned that you work for Ma Bell—any hope of our rates going down?" Obviously, such an approach would signal the respondents that the session is to be informal and freewheeling.

Another part of the session deals with the rules, or "Do's and Don'ts," of the session, and a general explanation as to the nature of group interviewing. A list of topics to be covered would include:

- Moderator/research company identification;
- brief statement of what a focus group is;
- respondents' representation of potentially thousands of others like themselves;
- no right or wrong answers, but rather, points of view;
- encouragement to speak out when holding a minority view;
- moderator has no vested interest in problem area (success or failure of product or service) but rather the responsibility of finding out what the respondents feel, say and do;
- no sales involved, strictly research;
- session is being recorded/monitored for purposes of the research;
- speak one at a time to avoid garbling on the tape;
- anonymity of client and respondents with no one held accountable for comments made.[35]

And, finally, it is usually advisable to give the respondents some idea of the scope of the interview and the general topics to be covered. This brief outline should allay their "fear of the unknown" as well as create a task-oriented atmosphere. There is a tendency for the moderator to get stale with the instructions and to ramble through them by rote. What must be remembered is that while it may be the moderator's 144th group session, it is the first for most of the members. The initial stage of the group must never be rushed over in order to get to what may be perceived as the more important tasks at hand.

Deciding on Style

The moderator should be very conscious of the overall manner or style in which the interview is conducted. The style adopted by the moderator will influence the interaction of the group and the nature of the resulting data. The following chart of *moderator styles* is a useful organization of the major approaches available.

		Involvement	
		Directive _____	*Non-directive*
	One of the Group	1 _____ 4	
Role	Play Dumb	2 _____ 5	
	Do a Job	3 _____ 6	

Along the horizontal axis is the directive/non-directive level of involvement. The directive portion describes a situation in which the moderator maintains strict control of the discussion. This high-involvement approach is an effort to keep the discussion orderly by closely following the moderator's guide. In contrast, the non-directive approach is a "hands off" style. The emphasis is on the group and the interaction between the group members. The moderator becomes involved only when the group wanders too far afield or hits a sticking point. The approach is much like that of a psychoanalyst who encourages the group members to continue their "self-exploration of an experience until some measure of clarity is attained."[36]

The other axis represents different types of roles that a moderator can create. For example, the "One of the Group" role is established when the moderator attempts to identify with the group and remove him or herself from an overt leadership role. The non-authoritarian approach creates an atmosphere in which everyone feels comfortable in expressing their opinions and is an appropraite climate when attempting to generate hypotheses or describe a set of attitudes toward common objects. The "Play Dumb" role is indicative of a situation in which the moderator alludes to the fact that he or she is "ignorant about the area and wants to learn more." It works well with professional people or when discussing complex issues. And finally, the "Do a Job" role befits a formal, serious, roll-up-your-sleeves session. It is useful when there are hard choices to be made: a new ad concept to evaluate or questionnaire to design.

Each of these roles can be conducted at either a directive or non-directive level of involvement; hence the style. For example, a moderator who adopts a "Play Dumb" role can take a high level (directive) of involvement by asking such questions as "I need you to explain that point a little more clearly for me?" or "I'm not sure, but I think we should move along to . . ." At a non-directive level, a "Play Dumb" role question might be "Perhaps you could help me to understand the way in which you . . .?"

It can be suggested that any moderator who approaches every group session with the same style will never be totally successful. The moderator style sets an important atmosphere in which the data are collected. It must change according to the nature of the group, the time allocated and the definition of the problem. Those moderators that adopt a middle-of-the-road approach and do not waiver from it will survive quite nicely. But is it the true expert of group dynamics who can overtly adapt their style to reflect the conditions at hand.

The Levels of Group Communication

The complexity of group interviewing becomes evident when one analyzes the nature of communication within a group session. Conducting a group interview necessitates that the moderator operates on at least seven different levels of communication—simultaneously![37]

First the moderator has to cover the guide, both the major points and the subpoints. Regardless of whether the moderator chooses a directive or non-directive level of involvement, the moderator is still responsible for generating information on all aspects of the moderator's guide. In a directive situation, the topic areas are covered sequentially with the moderator questioning the members until the first topic is exhausted; the moderator then proceeds to the next topic. The practice of "tracking" requires that any offf-the-immediate-track topics be discouraged and that efforts are devoted to keeping the conversation focused—in a "Do a Job" type of moderator role. In non-directive situations, the moderator's guide is much less rigidly interpreted and the moderator will usually let the discussion wander. If it jumps forward, the moderator doesn't interrupt, but simply makes a mental note of those issues that have been missed (and returns to them later).

In order to make sure that the topic areas are covered, the moderator must be aware of pace:

> Pacing an interview is much like writing an essay examination. The interviewer must assign an implicit weight to each question and move on, even if not entirely finished, when the question has taken

as much time as it is worth. Like an ideal examination, the ideal interview ends at the bell.[38]

There are several ways of doing this. One is to offer a summarization or wrap-up—"Let's see what we've covered so far." This closing of the loop provides the group with a chance to see just what they have accomplished and also signals an end to the topic. This approach lessens the perceived effect of being cut-off and, instead, makes a smooth and positive transition. A second technique is to call for a vote. As a tool the vote is useful because it implies that the discussion on a particular topic is over. It should be noted, however, that we are not about to digress into doing means and modes. In most situations the count is irrelevant—it is the symbolic value of taking a vote that is important.

A second level of communication is one at which the moderator attempts to involve all of the group members. While it is not necessary for each and every respondent to participate with equal frequency, the objective is to promote an active exchange of ideas and attitudes among group members. One technique to facilitate such an interaction is the ping-pong method. The moderator simply interjects "And what is your opinion?" If the moderator does this early in the session the members usually pick up the idea that they are encouraged to react to one another's comments.

In many instances such natural interaction does not occur; there is no easy interchange of ideas. One reason for this is that some people feel a lack of expertise in an area or are shy about articulating an opinion. They seem to sink back into the couch, pull back in their chairs, or simply give monosyllabic responses. Shy persons need encouragement and reassurance that their views are of value to the moderator and are acceptable to the group as a whole. Once an opinion has been elicited from a non-participant, it is extremely important that the moderator reinforces or rewards the effort. Such comments as "That's very interesting" or "That's an important point" will bolster the members' sense of security and reward them for actively participating.

At times there is a genuine expert in the group who unconsciously relegates everyone else to the position of nonexpert. Usually experts of this kind can be induced to refrain from group domination by saying to them when they pause for breath, "We'd like to get some other opinions about this matter." And, *turning* to another member saying "Steve, tell me how *you* feel about this advertisement?" Such negative reinforcement will normally induce the expert to be somewhat less vocal.

The pseudo-expert can be more of a problem. At times the "know-it-all" requires drastic action.

> The interviewer can cut him (or her) off in mid-phrase, ask pointedly if there are others who want to express an opinion, avoid eye contact with the pest, look bored, study the ceiling while the pest is speaking, pretend to have a severe headache, change the subject abruptly the second the pest has stopped talking, or display other signs of fatigue. Most pests can be controlled by such tactics but, alas, a few cannot. When an uncontrollable pest appears and has his (or her) way, the only consolation is that some group interviews are better than others. In most cases, it is illegal for a civilian to use Mace.[39]

Third, the moderator must introduce related points to stimulate thought and motivate discussion. With the directive level of involvement it is much easier for the moderator to interject a different line of reasoning or stimulating new idea. For example, he or she can ask "Perhaps we should discuss the area of nutrition" or "Let's try to think of as many different applications as we can." When operating on a non-directive level, however, new ideas should emerge spontaneously. Such natural inclinations are minimized under moderator prompting. If any stimulation or motivation is to be done in such a situation it must be done with extreme subtlety or not at all. If the group is lethargic or uncreative it may be a simple reflection of the topic and any prompting may result in *just* answers to questions.

At a fourth level of communication, the moderator must probe to get beyond the guide into the group's thoughts and feelings. The kind of question that is asked, how it is phrased, when it is asked, how it appears in context and the tone in which it is asked can all effect the kind of response generated. Usually, structured questions will result in standardized, socially acceptable responses. The question "Do you think nutrition is important in a breakfast cereal?" will evoke a positive reply. But conduct a test and you'll probably see that they can't distinguish B12 from a J24 or any other letter and number—nutrition is generally not a motivating factor in actual choice-making. Such hard-edged frontal questions rarely uncover true feelings. The responses are canned answers of appropriate social standing with little information value. If, however, we juxtapose a structured question next to an unstructured, we can see the potential value of coming at the issue indirectly:

Structured Question: From your personal knowledge of the candidates, do you think that Bush is more qualified in the area of foreign policy than Dole?

Unstructured Question: What impresses you most about any of the presidential candidates?

With the structured question, the moderator assumes almost total control. He or she has singled out the candidates to compare and the attribute on which to compare them. The unstructured question, in contrast, is " . . . one that does not fix attention on any specific aspect of the stimulus situation or of the response; it is, so to speak, a blank page to be filled in by the interviewee."[40]

One of the best unstructured questions may be the simple follow-up question, "Why?" The respondent is being forced to analyze his or her own rationalizations or explanations for an expressed attitude, belief, or behavior. With better moderators such questions become almost automatic: "How did you arrive at that conclusion?", "Why did you say that?" By continuing this probing, the moderator may be able to uncover feelings that were either not evident to the respondent or suppressed.

Fifth, the moderator must constantly think ahead to the next area of the guide; there may be the need to jump ahead of the guide if someone opens up a new topic. This is a matter of contingency planning. It is not enough to merely stay up with the group and respond or interject on current topics. The moderator must be mapping out where the conversation is heading and be in the position to anticipate problems.

The sixth level of communication is emotional. The moderator must be able to set an emotional tone that coincides with the makeup of the group members and the topic under investigation. The emotional tone of the group contributes to the context in which interaction takes place. The moderator should be able to manipulate the emotions of the group in order to generate the most appropriate environmental setting:

The emotionality of the group is a curious feature. Some are determined and sturdy, a buoyant conversation will go on as if it hardly

matters what the moderator does. Some groups are delicate and
fragile, needing wooing and encouragement. In other instances, the
chemistry is awful, a creeping lethargy takes hold, the liveliest
response is apathy, and the situation may be hopeless. Sometimes it
can be rescued by "blasting," that is, raising the most dramatic or
controversial aspect; by shifting gears and calling for a break; or be
confronting the problem by exploring why the group seems to be
uninterested. Not infrequently groups are over-stimulated, so giddy
with the novelty, the attention, the rewards, the social interaction,
their self-consciousness, or the absurdity of discussing some unlikely
topic for two hours, that a contagious hilarity takes hold, with exaggerated comments and hysterical laughter. These reactions need in-
terfering with, perhaps by shifting attention to something about the
physical arrangements, the taping, a comment about getting " back to
work" or again, examining the reaction itself, asking why the topic
seems so funny.[41]

And finally, the seventh level of communication requires that the
moderator constantly weigh the importance of what is being said, and
either encourage it to continue by probing and asking additional questions,
or terminate it gracefully. For the entire duration of a group session the
moderator is *continually* making intuitive judgments about the relative
merits of *continuing* on or changing directions. If a judgment is made to
continue it is with the belief that some additional understanding will take
place; that any additional mileage of information is worth the time and
energy it will take to generate it. In contrast, by moving on to another topic
area the belief is that either no additional information is available or that
the value of the information is not worth the effort to extract it.

OBSERVING THE GROUP

As group interviewing has increasingly become the consumer research
technique of the 1980s, more and more analysts, managers, directors, and
vice presidents have decided to "peer through the looking-glass." The
result can be a rather heady experience—real people expressing their
thoughts about *your* advertising concept or *your* new package design. The
strengths of the technique are quickly obvious to the observers. On the
other side of the mirror are consumers who are willing to tell you what

they think based upon their own experience, in their own language. Group dynamics can create insightful exhanges and a skillful moderator can probe for meaningful explanations. And the unique aspect of most group interviews is that this rich flow of data can be directly observed by decision-makers *as it happens*.

But observing should not be viewed as a comfortable spectator sport. There are some responsibilities that accompany the festivities. There are some observation skills that need to be detailed in order to make sense of the information, for as Alice remarked in *Through the Looking-Glass,* "Somehow it seems to fill my head with ideas—only I don't exactly know what they are!" In the same way, the following points by the Advertising Research Foundation need to be enumerated for observers in order to help them know exactly what to look for:

Observers should not expect every moment of the discussion to be meaningful, every question to work, or every response to be salient and quotable. Participants will be real people responding spontaneously.

Observers should not expect to experience a consensus within a group or among groups. Qualitative research is designed to generate a range of response, develop hypotheses and deepen understanding.

It is important for observers to listen carefully to what is being said. That is, to avoid selective listening to support a preconceived point of view, and to avoid projecting personal meaning and values to what is being said. In listening, it is important to be alert to shades of meaning and to word selection.

Observers should try to watch as well as listen. Nonverbal cues can sometimes be more meaningful than verbal responses.

During the discussion, observers should make notes of key impressions for discussion during the debriefing after the focus group.

Observers may want to ask for additional probes or to insert new questions during the discussions, or at the end of the session. Some moderators come to the viewing room before the session ends for such additional question areas. Other moderators prefer to have a note brought to them in the discussion room.[42]

While on the surface the idea of observing a group appears to imply a passive role for the observers, any such passivity is unfortunate and, potentially, dangerous. By not educating the observers on how to watch and how to listen, the researcher is just courting the disasters that can easily occur in this type of research. Would you have an amateur design a survey instrument or expect them to be able to use factor analysis to analyze the data? Of course not. But you will condone, and often encourage, that same amateur to make snap judgments based upon a few minutes of peering through the looking-glass. One researcher recently described such a problem:

In one experience I had several years ago, one of my clients wanted to begin marketing a product that was new to its product mix. Because excitement ran high at the company about the prospects for the product, the client developed a mental image of who the users were likely to be. Not surprisingly, the client envisioned highly educated people, probably with MBAs, upwardly mobile, well-dressed, and well-groomed. The client was not prepared for the construction workers, homemakers, and factory workers who legitimately used the product. I would venture to say that the client did not absorb one word of the focus groups as a result of the preconceived image of the users.[43]

ANALYZING AND REPORTING

The data which result from group interview research can be quite attractive. In addition to the rich, impressionistic feelings of individual respondents, there are also the many benefits derived from the group interaction: ideas bouncing off people, thoughts triggering additional responses with waves of intermingled opinions and attitudes. Yet the very richness and complex interactions of group data provide significant conceptual and practical problems for understanding and analysis. However, if one were to look at the literature on group interviewing, the issue of data analysis and reporting is virtually ignored. No one writes about it, no one talks about it. The question which seems to be ignored is, "Once we've got eight or ten hours of taped interviewing, what do we do with it?" A good group moderator knows that once the data have been collected, the real work begins. The ability to take large mounds of experiences, problems, successes, and biases and shape them into a decision-oriented report, *is* the thing that separates the professionals from the amateurs. Several qualitative researchers have summed up the frustrations involved:

> Qualitative data tend to overload the researcher badly at almost every point: the sheer range of phenomena to be observed, the recorded voulme of notes, the time required for write-up, coding, and analysis can become overwhelming[44]

> Analyzing depth interviews and group discussions is not easy. It takes up a lot of executive time and is tedious, tiring, and difficult. As a consequence, it is usually done very badly.[45]

> Methodologists obviously prefer to spend more time on such matters as gaining access, interviewing, choosing informants, handling reciprocities, and so on, rather than on the intellectual work of analysis.[46]

And finally, the apparent lack of concern about data analysis on the part of many qualitative researchers has been recently addressed by one internationally-active practitioner:

> The situation is rather like a quantitative researcher collecting information by means of questionnaires which he then quickly skims through and arrives at an interpretation of the data without any editing, coding or tabulation of the results. Data are data, whether they be in the form of numbers, words or whatever, and the principles of data analysis are the same irrespective of whether the data have been collected by quantitative or qualitative means.[47]

Before a review of qualitative data analysis techniques is undertaken, a few words need to be said about transcription. After many group sessions the initial step is to transcribe the audio taping into a typed version. The transcription of a session provides a permanent description of the "actual" wording and discussion. There are, however, several major drawbacks.

First, if the session is to be transcribed it is of utmost importance that the moderator keep secondary conversations to a minimum in the group interviews. Transcribing is almost impossible when everyone is talking at once—which can be the case unless the moderator keeps order. Second, the cost factor is not insignificant. Hours of secretarial time can be devoted to the task of creating a 40-50 page document. Third, the value of such an undertaking can be questioned. In spite of what we would like to believe, much of some group interview sessions is simply not worth transcribing.

Data Reduction

There are a number of overlapping activities that can go into data analysis. Data reduction is the process by which the researcher attempts to reduce the available information down to a more manageable, and therefore more meaningful, amount. It is an organization method that classifies data into parsimonious units. Two general approaches of data reduction have evolved; deduction and induction.

The term "deduction" refers to reasoning from the general to the specific. In our situation, we are interested in the process of data reduction from the general to the specific. This means that classification is accomplished by defining general areas of concern and then grouping the specifics accordingly. An analogy may help explain. A child comes home after Halloween and decides to organize the spoils of his or her masquerading. Our little friend's passion is jelly beans and so the sorting proceeds on the basis of identifying the really important issue at hand—separating the jelly beans from the rest of the candy. The next task is to categorize the jelly beans, and being an expert on the topic, the child follows a procedure of further categorizing by flavor (the raspberry ones are particulary tasty). The organizing scheme has been from the general to specific using a pre-set group of categories (jelly bean, non-jelly bean, raspberry, non-raspberry) to drive the data reduction operation (from all candy to raspberry jelly beans).

The qualitative researcher can proceed in much the same manner, using a set of predetermined, general categories to reduce and organize specific attitudes, opinions or observations. In some situations the researcher is interested in the answer to a defined research question. For example, in the group session on Travelers' Checks, one important research question had to do with effect that price had on the choice of which type of check to purchase. In the subsequent report it was noted that price was relatively unimportant and that "acceptance" by merchants was the key concern. Quotations were organized to support this conclusion:

"I'm just always afraid that I'll get in some store, stand in line for five minutes with an armful of stuff, and have the clerk refuse the check."

"If you're talking about $20 or $30 that's one thing, but usually the difference is only a couple of bucks. It's not worth shopping around."

"I don't even think about it [price]. It's just not that important."

At other times the general categories are not in the form of research questions but rather decision choices. In a group session on new prototype pen sets, a company was interested in consumer preferences for different types of bases—black glass versus lucite. With respect to their preference for a black glass base over lucite, male participants remarked about the lucite that:

"I don't like plastic."

"Lucite isn't heavy enough."

"The lucite surface is wavy."

The female participants generally preferred the lucite over the black glass. They preferred the lucite because:

"The glass will chip easily."

"The glass finger prints easily."

"Glass collects dust quickly."

The deductive approach to data reduction is most useful when the researcher enters the analysis stage with certain research questions in mind or definitive decisions to be made. The data are then distilled and described according to the categories or codes that were established.

In the inductive approach, the classification scheme is not imposed by the researcher; the categories emerge out of the data. Individual observations become the means by which an organization or typology evolves. In most situations this approach is used when the research problem is related to exploratory research or hypothesis generation. In this exploratory manner the emerging themes or patterns become analogous to the techniques of cluster and factor analysis. Specific observations are used to build toward general patterns. The categories that evolve can be of any sort; descriptions, attitudes, lifestyles, what have you. For example, the research department at D'Arcy, MacManus and Masius have successfully used the notion of "Belief Systems" to guide much of their advertising research. When doing group-interviewing sessions, one objective is to derive the key belief clusters from the data. The beliefs emerge from the subjective probing of group member's responses: identifying and organizing those beliefs that govern behavior. Some years ago, Masius was asked to look at the viability of making a corporate statement about the range of products marketed by Eden Vale in Britain. The group sessions were conducted in a non-directive fashion with the moderator facilitating a general discussion of the manufacturing, marketing and consuming of dairy products. Two conflicting belief clusters emerged from an analysis of the impressionistic data. One belief was that "manufacturing processes take some of the goodness out" and the second belief was that dairy products were "natural, good things." The analysis was done by pouring over the data and looking for commonalities, beliefs that kept on appearing in the dialogue. It should be noted that in this case a successful campaign ensued based on the the theme "Down at Eden Vale we do as little as possible. For your sake we know nature only needs a little help."[48]

Data Display

Whether the original data has been transcribed or not, and whether the method of reduction is deductive or inductive, there is still the practical problem of exactly how one goes about presenting the information; that is, the narrative text, quotations, tables, matrices, graphs, and so on. If the session has not been transcribed, the researcher will be obliged to sit down with the tape recorder, pencil, and paper and begin creating the filing system to be used. If, however, the session has been transcribed, filing can proceed according to what one researcher affectionately describes as the "Scissor and Sort" or "Long Couch, Short Hallway" technique.[49] The first step is to edit, code, or bracket the segments that will form the substance of the report. This can be done by a numbering system (a number refers to a specific theme, idea or concept) or a color system (underlining various dialogue with different colors representing the different categories). The next step is to cut each interview apart, bracket by bracket, number by number, and to sort the edited quotations by topic category (hence, a long couch or short hallway will do nicely). Another researcher describes the same process using videotapes:

> In a recent study of drinking habits we analyzed videotapes from eight group discussions. We had drawn up a set of questions prior to the groups and these were supplemented with further hunches developed by the moderators during the course of the discussions. These questions were set down in coded form on large sheets of paper and the tapes were played back. For each coded question we noted down where on the tapes the subject was discussed (using the tape counter) and the substance of the discussion. We also added further codes to our score sheet where these were needed. Then, taking each research question in turn, we were able to see immediately the main substance of the arguments put forward, and any differences across the groups.[50]

Tables and charts can be created by imposing a ranking system on the data. If, for instance, the amount of experience that consumers have in a product category is believed to effect their attitudes, a table can be created to investigate the hypothesis. By arranging the respondents comments by the amount of experience it may be possible to reveal a pattern. Data can also be displayed graphically. If you were interested in the differences between groups of respondents on two related dimensions, the data from each group could be scaled (for instance, rated as high, medium or low on the two dimensions) and then plotted in space with the two dimensions forming the axes.

Interpretations

The success or failure of qualitative research resides mainly in the interviewing and *interpreting* skills of the researcher. So far, all of the analysis and reporting described have involved a series of connected tasks; transcribing, categorizing, distilling, coding, bracketing and editing. Our report is purely descriptive. The question remains as to whether the researcher should stop at the point of faithful description or go beyond with interpretations, implications and suggestions. For example, the following excerpt is from a report done for Colonial Williamsburg.

There would seem to be an opportunity to promote the many different faces of Williamsburg—the fact that people come back again and again and experience Williamsburg with a different perspective. The different kinds of Williamsburg vacations at different stages of life was an interesting point of view expressed by some of the women who had come back several times. There would also seem to be an opportunity to "sell" Williamsburg at different seasons. Women who have been there at various seasons report that it is, indeed, a completely different kind of experience.[51]

Of course, the problem situation in this case was related to the "selling" of Colonial Williamsburg, in an advertising campaign, by enumerating the major selling points or the attributes that make it a unique vacation spot. The report was able to identify different kinds of experiences that consumers' perceived and, then, to extend that description to an interpretive level.

Whether the group interview report is interpretive or not is dependent upon many things: the relationship of research and management; the topic under discussion; the overall research design, and so on. But the basic report should be a fully descriptive analysis which blends summarizations with quotations. While it is fair to say that by the best of current standards, analysis of group data is a mysterious, half-formulated art, the report should come alive with feelings. As was mentioned in the beginning of this chapter, a major benefit of the group interview is that it provides data in a form with which everyone is familiar. It is not a series of cross-tabulations reported in a stark, dry format. Rather it is, or should be, a lively set of narrations, quotations, tables, and interpretations.

TRADE-OFFS

The compromises that must be made when choosing a research technique should be based upon the specific advantages and disadvantages of each. The strengths of group interviewing should be analyzed in terms of the information that is generated. It is this knowledge of what the technique has to offer which will also allow us to ascertain whether it is the appropriate technique to solve a particular problem. But while the advantages form the basis for understanding the capabilities of the technique, we cannot over-look the limitations. In fact, it is essential that we become as familiar with the weaknesses of an approach as we are with its strengths.

Strengths

Speed. If consumer information is used by decision makers as food for thought, then the group interview is the MacDonalds of consumer research cuisine. Large sample, quantitative surveys usually take weeks or even months for designing surveys, gathering data, coding responses and run-ning statistical analyses. Experimental designs are equally as cumbersome and slow-moving. In contrast, a three-or four-interview study can be con-ducted, analyzed and reported in less than a week in an emergency situa-tion. Several weeks is more "normal" turnaround for most studies. Certain-ly such time responsiveness is an appealing commodity in a dynamic en-vironment which is increasingly characterized by consumer fickleness, legal changes, and competitor incursions.

Flexibility. In spite of the rather exact descriptions of how to conduct group interviews formed in many articles and textbooks, the technique really has very few axioms. Instead, the procedure can be imaginatively adapted to suit different situations. In addition to the general design of the research study, each group meeting exemplifies the word "flexibility":

> A good group interviewer works from a list of topics—listening, thinking, probing, exploring, framing hunches and ideas as he proceeds. He also "listens with the third ear," trying to achieve a grasp and an intuitive understanding of what is being said. He looks at the respondents, watches posture, listens to voice tone, and tries to decide when respondents are "putting him on." He is not an automatic, mechanical, wind-up question asker, as survey inter-viewers necessarily and properly are.[52]

Empathy. The group interview can drastically reduce the distance be-tween the consumer who produces research information and the decision maker who uses it:

When was the last time you can recall a bank vice president talking to a mill worker or a school teacher about his or her financial concerns? There is an unfortunate tendency for most bankers to insulate themselves from the daily concerns and the individual feelings of their customers. While this is not a conscious effort, the result is, nonetheless, the same as if bankers purposely ignored their own clientele.[53]

In the banking example, the group interview setting is an ideal situation for bankers to see customers, not as average monthly balances, but rather as flesh and blood people with specific needs and concerns. It provides the vehicle within which bankers can watch and listen to individuals discuss a service, examine a seies of advertisements, contemplate a bank's image or criticize a new product idea. As such, the group interview is an invaluable touchstone, grounded in the thoughts and feelings of real consumers. Or as Woodrow Wilson once commented, "You get a great deal more light on the street than you do in the closet." You get a good deal more light by keeping your ears open among the rank and file of your fellow citizens than you do in any conceivable private conference.[54]

Subjectivity. If you are like most of us, you have been confronted with the task of filling out a questionnaire or responding to an interviewer's questions. Questions such as "How many years of formal education do you have?" or "Have you purchased Gizmo soap in the last three months?" are easy enough—a number and a yes/no response. However, when the question is "Are you satisfied with the quality of performances at the San Dimas Community Arts Program?" and the response format is of the "Very Satisfied" to "Very Unsatisfied" variety, you may feel a bit uneasy about your answer. Again, like most of us, you'd probably want to respond by checking the "Very Satisfied" box and writing in the margin, "If it wasn't for the uncomfortable seats in Section E," or perhaps "Very Unsatisfied....but several of the individual actors have been outstanding." The point, of course, is that many of our opinions and attitudes are not of a box-like nature. We do a lot of thinking in contingencies and while quantitative techniques follow the "no ifs, ands or buts" rule, the group interview is very good at handling all such contingencies. It does not impose a response structure on the individual members.

Dynamics. One of the most important strengths of group interviews is derived from group dynamics. Hess has described some of the potential beneficial effects:

Synergism: The combined effort of the group will produce a wider range of information, insight and ideas.

Snowballing: A bandwagon effect often operates in a group interview situation in that comments by one individual will often trigger a chain of responses from the other members.

Stimulation: After an initial wariness, the respondents get "turned on" in that they want to express their ideas and be a part of the group.

Security: The individual may find comfort in the fact that others' feelings are not greatly different from their own, and that they can expose an idea without necessarily being forced to defend or elaborate on it.

Spontaneity: Since no individual is required to contribute, their comments may be more spontaneous since they are responding because they want to, not because it is expected.[55]

The group provides the setting for an exciting interaction, an interplay of ideas and emotions among six data processing managers, eight purchasing agents or ten housewives.

Weaknesses

Artificiality. We have a tendency to think of a group intervied as an opportunity in which we are able to peek into consumers' minds—into their private lives. We must continually remind ourselves, however, that groups are staged, orchestrated research.

They are unnatural, not only to the group members who are asked to "spill their guts" in groups of 8 or 10, but also to the viewers who are engaging in a unique form of voyeuristic research.[56]

It is safe to say that people do not normally sit around and discuss the image of a political candidate, a new frozen food dessert, or the services of a major airline in little groups while sipping Coca-Cola. And yet because of the fact that we can see them, hear them patiently responding to questions, and giving seemingly intelligent answers, our natural cautions are minimized. As one research consultant has commented, "Make no mistake about it, focus groups are 'research's theater' and whether conscious or not, virtually all the participants are responding to the artificial environment and playing a role."

Posturing. There are several different aspects of the social event known as a "focus group" that lend themselves to a kind of social posturing. One of the most difficult problems with the social environment is the desire on the part of the group members to try to please the moderator. For example, we can get groups of housewives to sit around and discuss fruit cocktail labels for two hours. Does this signify that such labels play a meaningful part in these individuals' lives? The answer, of course, is no. But think of the process: the housewives are invited to attend a group session, given food and drink, paid money, and told that what they have to say is extremely important. In an effort to help out and respond to the *quid pro quo*, group members can become more concerned with telling you what they think you want to hear. True feelings, motives, and exact accounts of past or future behaviors get lost in the process.

A second social posturing effect is related to intelligence. A brief example is sufficient to illustrate the point. In a 1947 study by Gill[57], it was found that 70 percent of the respondents expressed an opinion about the "Metallic Metals Act" even though no such act had ever existed or been proposed. Most individuals, especially in a group setting of their peers, do not want to appear anything less than bright, witty and charming.

And finally, group members will not only tell you what you want to hear and what appears to be intelligent, they will also respond in a socially acceptable manner. Of course they read *Scientific American* rather than *Playboy*!

Selectivity. As we have seen, researchers and moderators are often faced with observers who use isolated responses that they hear in a group interview as confirmation of their own beliefs. For example, product managers do not always go into a group session with an open mind. Instead, they may be prepared to cue-in on individual responses that can be used as the basis for rationalizing a decision that has already been made. The resulting "selective listening" undermines the entire data analysis procedure. Group observers should take heed the words of J. Krishnamurti from *You Are The World,* "So when you are listening to somebody, completely, attentively, then you are listening not only to the words, but also to the feelings of what is being conveyed, to the whole of it, not part of it."

Compliance. A group session is a social interaction and as such exhibits the same set of rewards and sanctions that exist in a larger social system. The tremendous power of group pressure and compliance has been demonstrated in a series of studies now generally referred to as the Asch phenomenon. The basic Asch experiment is conducted as follows:

> Eight subjects are brought into a room and asked to determine which of three unequal lines are closest to the length of a forth line shown some distance from the other three. The subjects are instructed to announce their judgments publicly. Seven of the subjects are working for the experimenter and announce incorrect matches. The order of announcement is arranged so that the naive subject responds last. In a control situation subjects made very few incorrect matches. However, when another group of 50 naive subjects responded "after" hearing the unanimous but "incorrect" judgment of the other group members, 37 made a total of 194 errors, all of which were in agreement with the group's mistaken choice.[58]

Any veteran group moderator can describe the significant impact that several forceful individuals can have on others' responses. What may appear to an outside viewer as a unanimous group attitude may, in fact, be more reflective of social compliance than individual choice.

FINALITIES

The People of Earth

Perhaps the greatest strength of group interviewing is the mere fact that groups have unique characteristics. It has been noted earlier that certain group phenomena such as synergy and sponteneity can be very beneficial in the study of consumer behavior. But the real value of group interviewing may be best described in the opening paragraph of an article entitled "The Origins of Group Dynamics":

> If it were possible for the overworked hypothetical man from Mars to take a fresh view of the people of Earth, he would probably be impressed by the amount of time they spend doing things together in groups. He would note that most people cluster into relatively small groups, with the members residing together in the same dwelling, satisfying their biological needs within the group, depending upon the same source for economic support, rearing children, and mutually caring for the health of one another. He would observe that the education and socialization of children tend to occur in other, usually larger, groups in churches, schools, or other social institutions. He would see that much of the work of the world is carried out by people who perform their activities in close interdependence within relatively enduring associations. He would perhaps be saddened to find groups of men engaged in warfare, gaining courage and morale from pride in their unit and a knowledge that they can depend upon their buddies. He might be gladdened to see groups of people enjoying themselves in recreations and sports of various kinds. Finally he might be puzzled why so many people spend so much time in little groups talking, planning, and being "in conference." Surely he would conclude that if he wanted to understand much about what is happening on Earth he would have to examine rather carefully the ways in which groups form, function, and dissolve.[59]

Managerial Insights

Choose Carefully. In the corporate world it is a well known fact that excess profits attract new participants. Services are no exception. Given the current trend toward group interviewing it is not surprising that many new suppliers specializing in "focus-groups" have hung out their shingle. Many, if not most, are well-qualified. But this type of research needs to be held to the same type of rigorous standards as any other, including experimental designs. Messy data are no excuse for inconsistent and erroneous procedures. Many moderators are self-taught, with no background in social psychology, or marketers with no real-world experiences. In general, stay away from researchers or research companies that just do focus groups. If not, you will have a series of focus group reports sitting on your desk, regardless of whether or not that was the proper procedure to use.

For group moderators, maintain or expand your expertise in depth interviewing, projective and observation methods, and survey design and analysis.

Demand Strict Procedures. Group interviewing is in the process of developing a bad reputation. If everyone is not careful it will exhibit the same life-cycle characteristics that befell motivation research, and we will have a large number of little rooms with one-way mirrors sitting empty. Leo Bogart recently commented in an article entitled "Progress in Advertising Research?":

> The great appeal of the so-called "focus groups" in preference to the old one-on-one depth interviews is that you can take an hour with twelve people and claim twelve respondents instead of one. The sample looks almost respectable. Beyond that, when the interview goes on behind a one-way mirror, with the client looking on, his enthusiasm is almost guaranteed. What a revelation to see for yourself that there are live people out there who have actually heard of your product and have strong "no opinions" about it! At the moment of truth, you can virtually fling yourself through the glass and straighten out the respondent's foolish misperception of your product. This is good show business, and it's certainly good hypothesis-generation, but let's not kid ourselves that it's research.[60]

Specify The Sample. Greater control needs to be exerted in this area both by researchers and managers. The details of the recruiting process should be clearly enumerated; the characteristics of the sample need to be expressly defined. As we noted, there are some unique procedures that can be employed in the data analysis phase if the proper sample is developed. Categorization and ranking can be done if users/nonusers are included, or men/women, rural/urban, *et cetera*. Different market segments need to be defined and the differences in their perceptions probed. This can't be done after the fact if the sample is not properly conceived.

Exploit Its Flexibility. Each group session should be unique. The structure should vary according to the research problem. Questionnaires can be distributed, projective methods such as game playing and personnification can be used, and the group members can be observed for behavioral clues. Applications abound:

1. Identifying and assessing new product ideas.
2. Making product-related decisions such as packaging, brand name, and logo.
3. Creating advertising themes, copy, and illustrations.
4. Testing advertising concepts and finished copy.
5. Identifying and assessing sales promotion ideas.
6. Measuring reactions to pricing and distribution strategies.
7. Uncovering competitive programs.
8. Gaining insights about customer decision processes.
9. Generating hypotheses about market segmentation and product positions.
10. Understanding the reasons for answers to quantitative surveys.[61]

Cases

The following case histories are successful applications of the group interview technique:

1. An incumbent mayor of a large eastern city was in the beginning stages of a re-election campaign. Several issues which hadn't been present in the last election had become important in recent months and were developing as election issues. What was not clear was how the voters perceived the mayor to stand on these issues relative to the other candidates. A series of group interviews were held in different precincts in order to crystalize the key points of each issue and to explore the perceptions that the respondents had concerning the candidates. In addition, several different campaign themes revolving around these issues were discussed. The respondents discussed the credibility of each theme and how it "matched up" with the candidates' images.

2. The issue of increasing deposit and lending levels with corporations led a regional bank to conduct a series of group interviews. The market of interest was high technology and manufacturing firms which had been in

existence for less than ten years and with a sales volume of at least $2 million. The participants were chief financial decision-makers from these two industries and the specific goals of the research were as follows:

Isolate and define specialized financial services which emerging growth companies consider important, and determine why they are viewed as important.

Determine the criteria employed in selecting banking relationships.

Explore factors affecting bank loyalty.

Evaluate banks currently offering services which emerge as most significant to these companies, and assess perceptions of "large city banks" versus "smaller local banks."

Assess reactions to bank solicitations, and elicit recommendations regarding useful and successful banking representative calls.

3. An advertising agency has been handling a leading detergent account for twelve years. The staff periodically feels it runs out of creative ideas, or becomes stale on the account. The values of detergent are known, so that the essence of what has to be communicated is established . However, group interviews are held to generate fresh insight as to what is going on in consumer households, particularly among buyers and non-buyers of the product.

ENDNOTES

[1]Adapted from Abrams, Bill (1983), "American Express is Gearing New Ad Campaign to Women," *The Wall Street Journal,* (August 4), p. 23.

[2]Myers, John G., William F. Massy and Stephen A. Greyser (1980), *Marketing Research and Knowledge Development,* (Prentice-Hall: Englewood Cliffs), p. 211.

[3]Miles, Matthew B. (1979), "Qualitative Data as an Attractive Nuisance: The Problem of Analysis," *Administrative Science Quarterly,* 24 (December), p. 590.

[4]Goldman, Alfred E. (1962), "The Group Depth Interview," *Journal of Marketing,* 26 (July), p. 61.

[5]*Focus Groups: Issues and Approaches* (1985), (Advertising Research Foundation: New York), p. 3.

[6]Axelrod, Myril (1975), "Marketers Get an Eyeful when Focus Groups Expose Products, Ideas, Images, Ad Copy, Etc. to Consumers," *Marketing News,* (February 28), p. 6.

[7]Mitchell, Andrew A. (1981), "Focus Groups: Theory and Method," in *Association of Consumer Research Proceedings,* Andrew A. Mitchell (ed.), p. 52.

[8]Bogart, Leo (1986), "Progress in Advertising Research?," *Journal of Advertising Research,* June/July, p.14.

[9]Axelrod, Myril D. (1976), "The Dynamics of the Group Interview," in *Association of Consumer Research Proceedings,* Beverlee Anderson (ed.), p. 437.

[10]Wells, William D. (1976), "Group Interviewing," in *Handbook of Market Research,* Robert Ferber (ed.), (McGraw-Hill: N.Y.), p. 145.

[11]Bellenger, Danny N., Kenneth L. Bernhardt, and Jack L. Goldstucker (1976), *Qualitative Research in Marketing,* (American Marketing Association: Chicago), p. 10.

[12]Andrews, Amy (1977), "How to Buy Productive Focus Group Research," *Advertising Age,* (July 11), p. 128.

[13]Bellenger, et al, op. cit., p. 13.

[14]Adapted from: Langer, Judith (1978), "Clients: Check Qualitative Researcher's Personal Traits to get More; Qualitative Researchers: Enter Entire Marketing Process to Give More," *Marketing News,* (September 8), p. 22 and Axelrod, Myril (1976) op. cit., p. 441.

[15]Smith, Joan (1972), "Group Discussions," *Interviewing in Market and Social Research*, (Routledge and Kegan Paul: Boston and London).

[16]Calder, Bobby (1977), "Focus Groups and the Nature of Qualitative Marketing Research," *Journal of Marketing Research*, 14, p. 353.

[17]Bellenger, et al, op. cit., p. 8.

[18]Ibid.

[19]Sampson, Peter (1972), "Qualitative Research and Motivation Research," in *Consumer Market Research Handbook*, Robert M. Worchester (ed.), (Maidenhead, England: McGraw-Hill Co.), p 7.

[20]Hess, John M. (1968), "Group Interviewing," in R.L. King (ed.), *New Science of Planning*, (American Marketing Association: Chicago), p.194.

[21]Payne, Melanie S. (1976), "Preparing for Group Interviews," in *Association for Consumer Research Proceedings*, Beverlee Anderson (ed.), p. 434.

[22]Yalom, Irvin D. (1970), *The Theory and Practice of Group Psychotherapy*, (Basic Books, Inc: New York), p. 215.

[23]Fern, Edward F. (1982), "The Use of Focus Groups for Idea Generation: The Effects of Group Size, Acquaintanceship, and Moderator on Response Quantity and Quality," *Journal of Marketing Research*, 19 (February), p. 1.

[24]Pope, Jeff (1977), "Six Ways to Improve Today's Focus Group Research," *Advertising Age*, July 11, p. 150.

[25]Libresco, Joshua D. (1987), "Disguise as Quantiative Research is Dangerous Abuse of Focus Groups," *Marketing News*, 21, (March 13), p. 2.

[26]Payne, op. cit., p. 436.

[27]Wells, op. cit., p. 137.

[28]Payne, op. cit., p. 436.

[29]Bernstein, Donald (1978), "Video TAT Solves Two Problems, Makes Focus Groups More Effective," *Marketing News*, (September 8), p. 11.

[30]Cunningham, Lynn and Kathy Tiffany (1987), "Anonymous Ranking Adds Dimension to Focus Groups," *Marketing News*, 21, (January 2), p. 53.

[31]Malone, Mike (1987), "Response Analyzer Designed to Enhance Focus Groups," *Marketing News*, 21, (January 2), p. 38.

[32]Lautman, Martin R. (1981), "Focus Groups: Theory and Method," *Association for Consumer Research Proceedings*, Andrew A. Mitchell (ed.), p. 55.

[33]Payne, op. cit., p. 434.

[34]Smith, Alexa (1986), "Researchers Must Control Focus Groups—and Those Behind the Mirror as Well," *Marketing News*, 20, (September 12), p. 33.

[35]Buncher, Martin M. (1982), "Focus Groups Seem Easy to Do and Use, But They're Easier to Misuse and Abuse," *Marketing News,* (September 17), p. 14.

[36]Merton, Robert K., Marjorie Fiske, and Patricia L. Kendall (1956), *The Focused Interview*, (The Free Press; Glencoe IL), p. 13.

[37]Adapted from Levy, Sidney J., unpublished manuscript.

[38]Wells, op. cit., p. 141.

[39]Wells, op. cit., p. 142.

[40]Merton, et al, op. cit., p. 15.

[41] Levy, Sidney J, (1979), "Focus Group Interviewing," in *Focus Group Interviews: A Reader*, James B. Higginbottom and Keith K. Cox (eds.), (American Marketing Association: Chicago), p. 36.

[42] *Focus Groups: Issues and Approaches*, op. cit., p. 17.

[43] Smith, Alexa (1986), "Researchers Must Control Focus Groups—and Those Behind the Mirror as Well," *Marketing News*, 20, (September 12), p. 33.

[44] Miles, Matthew D. (1979), "Qualitative Data as an Attractive Nuisance: The Problem of Analysis," *Administrative Science Quarterly*, (December), p. 590.

[45] McDonald, C.D.P. and W.A. Blyth (1978), in J.P. May (ed.), "Qualitative Advertising Research—A Review of the Role of the Researcher," *Journal of the Market Research Society*, 20, Number 4, p. 213.

[46] Sieber, Sam D. (1976), "A Synopsis and Critique of Guidelines for Qualitative Analysis Contained in Selected Textbooks," *Project on Social Architecture in Education*, (Center for Policy Research: New York).

[47] Griggs, Steve (1987), "Analysing Qualitative Data," *Journal of the Market Research Society*, 29, (January), p. 17.

[48] Reid, Tom (1981), "The Key That Can Turn On Buyers," *Marketing*, November 4, p.39.

[49] Wells, op. cit.

[50] Griggs, op. cit., p. 21.

[51] The Colonial Williamsburg Foundation, used with permission.

[52] Wells, op. cit., p. 134.

[53] Seymour, Daniel T., (1983), "The Trade-Offs of Focus Group Research," *Bank Marketing*, April, p. 20.

[54]Wilson, Woodrow, in *Woodrow Wilson Selections for Today*, Arthur Bernon Tourtellot (ed.).

[55]Hess, op. cit.

[56]Seymour, op. cit.

[57]Gill, S. (1947), "How Do You Stand on Sin?," *Tide*, March 14, p. 72.

[58]Adapted from S.E. Asch, 1958 "Effects of Group Pressure Upon the Modification and Distortion of Judgments," in *Readings in Social Psychology*, E.E. MacCoby et al. (eds.), (Holt, Rinehart and Winston: New York), pp. 174–183.

[59]Cartwright, Dorwin and Alvin Zander (1968), "Origins of Group Dynamics," in *Group Dynamics*, Dorwin Cartwright and Alvin Zander (eds.), (Harper and Row: New York).

[60]Bogart, op. cit.

[61]Welch, Joe L. (1985), "Researching Marketing Problems and Opportunities with Focus Groups," *Industrial Marketing Management*, 14, p. 250.

CHAPTER FIVE

DEPTH INTERVIEWING

To the uninitiated, interviewing is just "talking to people." And in many respects the interview is nothing more than a conversation: both typically involve a face-to-face verbal exchange of information, ideas, opinions, or feelings and contain messages exchanged through non-verbal as well as verbal channels of communication. An interview, however, is a specific kind of conversation directed to a definite purpose other than satisfaction in the conversation itself.

In 1985 a New Mexico vineyard was interested in deciding upon a name for its soon-to-be-released white wine. After much creation and elimination, the management of the company decided on its first choice, "Blue Teal," but was hesitant to finalize the choice without obtaining consumer comments. Management originally chose Blue Teal, which is the name of a duck, because of its potentially broad appeal—especially to men. Because men drink less wine than women, it was thought that a more masculine name would put more men at ease with a glass of wine. In-depth interviews were conducted with 35 very busy upscale consumers whose incomes were $25,000 or higher. To provide a comparison, three alternative names were presented to respondents along with Blue Teal. Two of the choices represented traditional wine names, one in French and two others in English. Management was interested in information about name memorability, perceptions, and positive versus negative associations of the name Blue Teal and the alternatives. Interviews revealed that women, as well as men, felt comfortable with the name. One fear, the association of Blue Teal with a duck, was not confirmed during the interviews. Although animal names abound in the domestic wine market (Stag's Leap, American Eagle, Cygnet Cellars) and seem to be in vogue, the research revealed that the positive association was mainly due to soft linguistic sound of Blue Teal.[1]

If the purpose of the Blue Teal interviews is to be achieved, several additional things must happen. One participant must assume and maintain responsibility for directing the interaction (asking questions) toward a goal, and the other participant must attempt to facilitate achievement of the purpose by following the direction of the interaction (answering questions). Over 40 years ago, R.C. Oldfield incorporated these attributes in his definition of the interview:

> Four main characteristics, then, jointly mark off what we should ordinarily call an interview from other types of human encounter. It is a meeting of individuals face to face; it is dedicated to a particular purpose, and is embarked upon with the consciousness of this; it employs true conversation; and there is frequently a non-reciprocal relation between the individuals taking part.[2]

In the area of consumer research, the interview technique is a tool used to gather personal information on marketing and advertising concerns. As described in Chapter One, depth interviewing is the first qualitative technique that we have seen that has the capability to penetrate the Outer-Self level of reasoned justifications and rationalizations. The charteristics of depth interviewing are such that the researcher is able to obtain an understanding of the subject at an Inner-Self level of meaning—a level that is usually concealed to the outside world and deals with introspections and elaborations. As such, the depth interview is an invaluable research technique in studying marketing and advertising problems. Unfortunately, in consumer research little emphasis has been placed on the basics of the technique in spite of its rather lengthy list of credentials in other disciplines:

Clinical Psychology: Interviewing is the principal diagnostic and therapeutic tool of modern psychiatry. Menninger, Mayman and Pruvser trace the psychiatric interview back to the year 2600 B.C.[3]

Sociology: Riesman and Benney have written on the history of the interview from the perspective of sociology. They describe its development from the diplomatic encounters between heads of state during the post-Renaissance period: through its introduction by Horace Greeley as a method useful to newspaper men: through its use by Mayhew, Booth and LePlay in understanding the working classes of the newly developing industrial society.[4]

Anthropology: Anthropologists have studied the development, differences, and demise of cultures using the interview procedure. Osgood, for example, reconstructed the Ingalik culture pattern on the basis of interview data provided by a sole surviving member.[5]

Since antiquity, the interview has been used professionally by philosophers, physicians, educators, priests and attorneys. In most respects the interviewing process and purpose remains the same across such diverse applications. What changes is the specific nature of the information collected: the lawyer seeks from his clients and witnesses information that may serve as legal evidence; the physician seeks from his patient information that will lead to a better diagnosis; the newspaper reporter seeks information to get all the relevant facts in a story or to lead him to further sources; and the market researcher seeks consumer information that will help to design, advertise, and distribute a product.

The real value of the interview technique is evident when one looks at the major common denominator across all applications. Information is derived from a single individual, with the implicit assumption that such information is unique. This stands in contrast to a more commonly held portrayal of society based upon stereotyping. Because people can fulfill similar functions and act in generalizable ways, they can necessarily be grouped in large categories. Such stereotyping or classification owes its existence to an economizing principle of the human intellect. It is easier to treat whites, professors, housewives, truck drivers and children as homogeneous groupings since it does not require us to explore individual differences. This orientation, then, concentrates on deriving commonalities or generalities. The emphasis is on what is similar. The interview technique, though, is not concerned with the process of generalizing to a larger population. The unit of analysis begins and ends with the individual—no subsequent stereotyping is necessary for the interview to be labeled a success.

These two extremes of inquiry—one concentrating on similarities and the other on dissimilarities—have been epitomized in two popular novels.

In 1932 Aldous Huxley described a foolproof system of eugenics designed to standardize the human product in *Brave New World*. The satirization of "the masses" was spelled out in the Bokanovsky Process:

One egg, one embryo, one adult—normality. But a bokanovskified egg will bud, will proliferate, will divide from eight to ninety-six buds, and every bud will grow into a perfectly formed embryo, and every embryo into a full-sized adult. Making ninety-six human beings grow where only one grew before. Progress.[6]

The benefit of this mass production was seen to be a standardized social order of millions of identical twins—easy to manipulate and easy to manage. Much the same can be said for our tendencies in research to want to simplify or minimize individual differences by stereotyping or concentrating on generalizations.

The more difficult extreme of analyzing individual differences is characterized by an interview which Studs Turkel had with a steelworker in *Working:*

> I would like to see a building, say, the Empire State, I would like to see on one side of it a foot-wide strip from top to bottom with the name of every bricklayer, the name of every electrician, with all the names. So when a guy walked by, he could take his son and say, "See, that's me over there on the forty-fifth floor. I put the steel beam in."

> I worked for a trucker one time. And I got this tiny satisfaction when I loaded a truck. At least I could see the truck depart loaded. In a steel mill, forget it. You don't know where nothing goes.[7]

The interview technique, regardless of the discipline in which it is applied, is unique as a methodology for discovering uniqueness about individuals. In spite of the fact that the trend has been toward large sample telephone and mail surveys with multivariate data analyses, the depth interview remains as a pre-bokanovskified research tool. It thrives on differences. Returning to our vineyard example for a moment, one of the main attractions of depth interviewing versus another technique, such as group interviewing, was the desire to explore idiosyncratic differences. The specific associations that individuals had to the intended brand name was the key element in management's mind. Whether it is Blue Teal or the Ingalik culture, the depth interview is a methodology for exploring the personal feelings of individuals.

THE INTERVIEWING PROCESS

The depth interviewing technique is a purposeful, and somewhat exhausting, approach to generating information. The intent of this section is to define the strategies and tactics needed to generate information that will address marketing and advertising concerns.

Preparation

The initial task, as always, is to go through the process of defining the management problem. Once this problem-driven analysis has taken place, the next step is to translate the management problem into a research problem. Different researchers have different methods for doing this translation. One method is as follows:

> I write the words "What do you want to know?" on a piece of paper. Below this I list my answers to this question. I ask my client to give his answers to the question also. Sometimes I'll have 20 things that I want to know. To put the list in proper order I first join those ideas that are similar or close, and I'll keep the rest. I will examine the list and test each to determine how each is related to the other questions. This is a search to see which questions are dependent on other questions for their solutions. After I have determined the order of importance I will rewrite the list putting the most important questions at the top and the others in descending order. This will usually solve the problem because the number one question will be the purpose of the study and the other questions will be the objectives. If we find answers to the objectives, we will have fulfilled the purpose. This list serves another need: the objectives become the question guide. Since they are now in order of importance they need only be rearranged into topic areas and reexamined to see if everything we want to know is fully covered. We can examine this organized list and add additional questions.[8]

Whether one chooses to use this method or another is not critical. Rather, what is important is that the researcher apply some defined logic to assure that the translation (from management problem to research problem) is accurate and thorough.

The question guide, which should be the output of this preparatory stage, can have a range of formats from a number of specific questions to a checklist of topics to be covered. The form of the question guide is largely dependent on (1) the length of interview and (2) the type of inquiry. Typically, the shorter interviews do not have time for probing or non-directive styles. A question is asked, an obligatory "Why do you feel that way?" is thrown in, and the interviewer pushes on to the next question. With longer interviews of one-half hour and up, the interviewer is much more inclined to let the respondent wander. A non-directive approach is not going to be saddled with pages of questions, but rather will depend upon a checklist in order to ensure that all topics are covered. In a similar manner, the type of research will influence the question guide. Exploratory (or hypothesis-generating) research studies are relatively unstructured, with a checklist being sufficient. However, conclusive research (which provides the evidence from which the decision maker can conclude which course of action to take) is more likely to need a specific set of structured questions.

Because of the nature of the management problem in our vineyard example, (positive vs. negative association of Blue Teal) it would follow that the interview guide would be fairly structured. Again, conclusive research requires a more tightly formatted approach.

Introductory Phase

The introductory phase of a depth interview has three objectives. The first objective is to convey required information from the interviewer to the respondent. There are a number of established information components:

1. *The purposes of the interview.* It is especially important that those purposes of the interview that may relate to the respondent's own goals and values be apparent to him.

2. *The ways in which information he contributes is to be used.* For example, if the respondent's statements are to be confidential, this must be known. If they are to be made available to other persons or incorporated in a publication of some sort, the respondent should know these facts.

3. In a general way, what will be expected of the respondent in the course of the interview. This means that the respondent should have some idea of the length of the interview, of whether or not any degree of expertness is required of him, whether he is to report actual information or to communicate his own attitudes and feelings, and the like.[9]

Such information is critical to almost every interview because it defines the expectations involved. With the respondents' role(s) being enumerated, most insecurities are minimized. It is also wise at this point for the interviewer to ask if the respondent has any questions. This final act will usually signal the respondent that the interviewer is a concerned individual, interested in what they think.

A second objective follows directly out of the first. The first minute of the interview is critical since during this time the respondent will decide how useful and interesting the session is likely to be for him or her. Therefore, the prevailing climate for the entire interview is usually established in the very first stage: the handshake, the arrangement of the chairs and the statement of objectives are all part of the interviewer/respondent rapport. And finally, the introduction also serves as a transition stage to move the respondent from the obligatory introduction to the body of the interview. One or more lead-in questions will do this and should be carefully thought out in advance by the interviewer. Even in a highly structured interview session, the interviewer should carefully devise the first questions. Typically, the most general questions and/or the least sensitive questions should be asked first.

Wording and Phrasing

The words and phrases used in a question are the smallest controllable elements of the depth interviewing process. The interviewer has his or her choice of every single word that is used to interact with the respondent. But how important can such decisions be—whether to use this word or that word? A few examples might shed some light on the topic:

In the recent Burger King/McDonald's comparative advertisements, Burger King claims that their flamebroiling was preferred over McDonald's frying by a margin of three to one. The key question was "Do you prefer your hamburgers flame-broiled or fried?" Leo Shapiro, an independent researcher, decided to ask the question another way: "Do you prefer a hamburger that is grilled on a hot stainless-steel grill or cooked by passing the raw meat through an open gas flame?" The results to this question had 53 percent of the people preferring the McDonald's grilling process.[10]

Elmo Roper, preparing to make a poll for Fortune magazine on attitudes toward governmental attempts to keep peace, pretested the following question: "Should the United States do all in its power to promote world peace?" Ninety-seven percent of the answers were in the affirmative. With a similar sample of respondents, the questions "Should the United States become involved in plans to promote world peace?" was responded to in the affirmative by only 60 percent of those questioned.[11]

The problem of constructing questions is essentially the problem of translating the objectives of the study into the concrete stimuli that will determine the nature of the resulting information. It is obvious from the examples just given that the "concrete stimuli" can be organized in many different ways, with the possibility that each arrangement will generate a different response. Following are seven major concerns which the interviewer should have in mind when formulating questions. Most of these are expressed as problems: problems that can be overcome if the interviewer is aware of how difficult it is to ask a good question.

Problem One: Why Did You Do That?

A temptation which besets interviewers is to translate the research objectives into questions too directly. If an objective of the research is to find out something about the determinants of a given attitude or behavior, the interviewer may ask "Why did you do that?" or "Why do you feel like that?" Simply asking the interviewee to provide insights about the determinants of his or her own behavior may be more than we can hope for. Frontal assaults in the form of very direct questions will typically generate answers. But the more inventive strategy of "flanking" the research objective will generally produce more thoughtful and valid responses. For example, if you were in the process of introducing a new medical product, you might do a series of depth interviews with doctors. At some point in the interview a logical question might be developed along the lines of "What product do you currently use to combat pellagra?" The obvious follow-up question would be to ask "Why that?" It may not be immediately apparent to the doctor why he prescribes that particular product versus some other. Consequently, it may be a more rewarding beginning to ask

"How long have you been prescribing that product?" or "Are there circumstances in which you would not prescribe that specific product?"

Problem Two: Openness versus Closedness

Questions, regardless of their length or subject matter, contain expectations of the length of response necessary for adequate coverage. Open questions elicit longer, more elaborate answers—they call for an explanation. Compare these open versus closed questions and then contrast the nature of the responses:

"How did you feel after test-driving the Alfa Romeo?"

"You felt great after test-driving the Alfa Romeo, didn't you?"

"What's the matter with the advertisement?"

"You don't seem to like the advertisement. Is it acceptable?"

The open question allows the respondent full scope; the closed question limits the respondent to a specific answer. The open question solicits views, opinions, motivations, feelings; the closed question usually demands cold facts only.

Problem Three: Antecedents

The antecedent of a question is something that the interviewer infers from a previous question or comment by the interviewee. Not every question has an antecedent. The opening question of the interview does not contain an antecedent, nor does any subsequent question which enters a new subject area unconnected with any previous discussion. Antecedents are important in question construction for two major reasons. First, they link together the interview questions in a continuous, logical process; for example:

Q: We've discussed the style of the car, now what do you think of its price?

The antecedent is the previous 'style' issue. The interviewer appears to be following a cohesive outline. And second, the antecedent can be important to reinforcing the respondent:

Q: Earlier you said you liked cars with very sleek lines. What's your opinion of this car?

By linking questions to what the respondent has said, the interviewer demonstrates that he or she has been listening to the respondent and is concerned with the answers, not just rushing through a series of questions.

Problem Four: Ambiguity and Misperception

The language in the question must conform to the vocabulary level of the respondent. Using words that are unknown or unclear to the respondent will result in invalid responses and alienation of the respondent. Linguists estimate that the average American adult knows fewer than ten percent of the words in the English language. And even those that they do know can mean many different things. The ambiguity of words or a sentence can result in the interviewer asking one question and the respondent answering quite a different question. The interviewer must be constantly aware of the alternative meanings given to words and the possibility of misinterpretation. The key is to avoid being a well-known, narrow-minded character from Lewis Carroll's *Through the Looking Glass:*

"When I use a word," Humpty Dumpty said in a rather scornful tone, "it means just what I choose it to mean—neither more no less."

This inattention to detail, caused by narrow thinking, can be disastrous. A classic case was reported by McNemar in 1946 when he asked rural Southerners if they favored "government control of profits." Feelings were overwhelmingly negative, since most of these respondents felt that "prophets" should be regulated only by the Lord.[12]

Problem Five: Leading Questions

The term "leading questions" refers to any question that is worded or phrased so that it appears to the respondent that the interviewer desires or expects a certain answer. For example, questions designed to elicit general attitudes toward advertisements directed toward children might read, "How do you feel about children's advertisements?" Different forms of the same question that are leading are "You wouldn't say that you were in favor of children's advertisements, would you?" and "Would you say that you are in favor of advertising directed toward children?" The ill effects of leading questions can be seen in an interesting courtroom scenario where a witness's legal testimony is interrupted by the opposition objecting to a leading question.

> Such are the forked questions habitually put by some counsel if unchecked, as "What was the plaintiff doing when the defendent struck him?" The controversy being whether the defendent did strike. A dull or a forward witness may answer the first part of the question and neglect the last.[13]

The interviewer will usually not engage in such blatant leading but inflection or casual wording can influence the respondent. The result being that the responses have a tendency to reflect the views of the interviewer rather than the unbiased opinions of the respondent.

Problem Six: Loaded Questions

Emotionally-charged words or stereotypes will influence the respondent's view of the situation:

> Steve Baumann, a wealthy New York-based real estate developer, is interested in obtaining a zoning variance in order to convert elderly housing into luxury apartments. Do you approve or disapprove of this zoning variance?

Words like "wealthy," "elderly," and "luxury" are laden with moral, spiritual and ideological values. A more relevant and more subtle example was provided earlier in the chapter by Leo Shapiro's comparison of Burger King and McDonald's—"open-gas" is somewhat less appealing than "flame-broiled," just as "fried" is less appealing than "grilled."

A final point should be made: during the course of a depth interview, there is a certain amount of learning going on. That is, while isolated cases of leading, loading and ambiguity might have minimal impact on the overall interview, the individual effects are cumulative—respondents do learn.

For instance, if the interviewer often phrases the questions around previous answers of the respondent, that respondent will become more open, trusting and cooperative. The respondent has learned that his or her opinions are important. In contrast, if the research is constantly using non-reinforcing words, the respondent may become disheartened, closed, untrusting and uncooperative.

Problem Seven: Sequencing

Within the interview session it is important for the questions to be properly ordered. In general, the sequence should be planned to make the interview as meaningful as possible; to give it a beginning, a middle, and an end. The initial questions should serve to engage the respondent's interest without threatening or taxing him or her before the interview has really begun. The most demanding or sensitive questions should be later in the interview so that if they trigger a refusal to continue, relatively little information is lost.

The body of the interview can follow two general procedures with the first being referred to as the "funnel sequence." The term describes a method of asking the most general or unrestricted questions at the beginning of a topic area and following that with successively more narrow or defined questions. The purpose is to prevent early questions from conditioning or biasing the respondent's later answers and to establish a context within which specific facts are related. If we were concerned with relating peoples' lifestyles to the magazines they read, we could "funnel" in the following manner:

Q 1. What kind of leisure activities do you engage in, and why?

Q 2. Of all of these activities, which one is the most important or enjoyable for you?

Q 3. Do you do much reading?

Q 4. How about magazines?

Q 5. Do you read the *U.S. News* and *World Report*?

In the first question, we have established total freedom in the discussion of the topic area. There are no antecedents or clues as to what is an "appropriate" answer. The second question requires the respondent to rank order mentally all of these activities while the third question is concerned with one specific activity. The fourth and fifth questions are even more narrow.

The "inverted funnel" is a pattern of narrower questions followed by broader ones. The main advantage of this approach is that it offers the respondent the building blocks for abstraction. It is especially helpful with topics in which the respondent has low involvement and, therefore, may not have an established general opinion. We may be interested in doing an image study, for instance on the University of Rhode Island library. We might lead the respondents through specific questions regarding the hours, personnel, availability of books, and so on, ending with the most general query, "Now taking all these things into consideration, what do you think of the University of Rhode Island library?"

PROBING

In Chapter One an analogy was drawn between qualitative research techniques and the tools used in paleontology. The analogy illustrated the vast differences in capability and purpose of the tools, using measures of cubic yards and jackhammers in the initial stages of the project and calipers, magnifying glasses and dental picks in the latter stages. The group interview technique was shown to have the ability to "dig below the surface" of standardized survey responses via the dynamics of small group interaction. Focus group data, however, are still largely the Outer-Self. Individuals are cautious that the responses they give are intelligent and socially acceptable. People are often not willing to discuss more closely-held elaborations:

> Most people have only the vaguest ideas about the reasons for their actions, such as what makes them buy a particular product. Buying actions, just like any other actions, are motivated by a whole group of different factors and very few people have the necessary insight to know what all these factors are and to assess their relative importance. Even when they do know them, they frequently are not prepared to reveal them in answer to a direct question. Very few

women will tell you that they buy a face cream because they want to be like the film star in the advertisement, and very few men will tell you that they buy a certain make of car to show off to their friends. In any case, very few people will admit that advertising has influenced their buying decisions. In all the surveys that have ever been done on this matter it has been found that a great number of people say that they take no notice of advertising, or that they were not influenced by it. This is clearly not the case.[14]

The 'probe' is the key skill involved in interviewing because it is the tool that enables the researcher to generate a different kind of information, information which suggests why someone has an attitude or behavior. It goes beyond mere description or surface explanation in an attempt to understand the cause of things that can explain behavior.

Probing is done at the discretion of the interviewer; he or she decides whether the responses are adequate to meet the research objectives. If not, the interviewer must decide on the nature of the inadequacy and then formulate a probe designed to uncover additional relevant information. It is also important, however, to emphasize that probing should not be indiscriminant. One should not fall into the trap of trying to probe deeper and deeper when there are no depths to probe. The result can be wasted time, redundant data, or an irritated respondent (which hardly facilitates good communication). For instance:

Q: You never go see a play?
A: Only occasionally, when somebody offers me a ticket but I never buy them.

Q: You never buy them?
A: No, I never buy them, because I really don't enjoy the theatre enough to spend the money.

Q: How come?
A: Well, as I just said, I don't enjoy it that much.

Obviously, this is a dead end and any further probing along this line will not result in further enlightenment. The probing aspect of a depth interview, then, is a delicate art of knowing (1) when to push for more information, (2) how to elicit the response—and, of course, when to realize that it is time to pull back and pursue another line of inquiry, and (3) how to interrupt.

When to Push

There are several types of situations in which probing is necessary. One of the most obvious is in a situation in which there is a need for additional clarification. The respondent's initial answer may be vague or the meaning unclear. It may be necessary to ask the respondent to rephrase their answer or provide specific examples. The interviewer, therefore, must use the advantages of the depth interview to his or her benefit by making sure that every topic is "nailed down" before moving on. The interviewer should also be prepared to probe for an elaboration. In this situation the interviewer is cognizant of the meaning behind the respondent's answer; however, the research objective requires a more detailed level of understanding. The probes are necessary to let the respondent know that the preceding response is not adequate.

A final situation is the use of probes to reinforce positively the respondent, to encourage a continuing dialogue on a topic. This probe is non-directional since it doesn't infer what the respondent should talk about, but it does suggest that the interviewer expects the respondent to continue.

How to Elicit

Encouragement is necessary to maintain communication and move the conversation in a direction which will satisfy the research objectives. It also expresses the empathetic understanding of the interviewer and reinforces the notion that the interviewer is indeed "listening." Verbal remarks include such things as: "I see," "Really," "Is that so!" Even the seemingly inane "Mm-hm" is saying to the respondent "Go on, continue, I'm with you: I'm listening and following you." Non-verbal communication is also very important—a nod of the head or an expectant facial expression are communication cues that will reinforce the verbal encouragements of the interviewer. A more specific non-verbal technique is the process of "mirroring." The interviewer can slowly adopt the physical mannerisms of the respondents by mirroring the way they sit in their chairs, talk with their hands, and so on. Such subtle moves can significantly reduce the psychological distance between the interviewer and the respondent, with the resulting atmosphere being more conducive to communication flow.

How to elicit elaborations is undoubtedly the most difficult task in the depth interview. It is almost as if the respondent and interviewer were locked into a very serious game of chess. The interviewer is on the offensive, trying to push deeper and deeper into the respondent's psychological territory. The interviewer probes until he or she meets resistance, then pulls back and tries elsewhere. The respondent offers unconscious and, at times, conscious resistance to the idea of being "invaded." The interviewer must proceed very delicately in order to probe to the level of understanding which is necessary, while at the same time not alienating the respondent.

The most logical way of encouraging elaboration would be to ask the simple question, "Why?" It is quick, efficient and gets at one of the basic facts which are necessary for truly understanding a phenomenon. The little word "why" symbolizes our inquiry into the reasons that motivate a particular attitude or behavior. However, even though we want the respondent to explain a point by self-analysis (Why do I behave this way?), it is generally agreed that the question "Why?" should be avoided. The reasons are twofold. First, it tends to make respondents feel as though they are undergoing police interrogation. Today, the word "why" can connote disapproval, displeasure; there are overtones of accusation that infer that you should account for your behavior. And second, Paul Lazarfeld, in his classic article "The Art of Asking Why?," has shown the amount of ambiguity involved in the word "why."[15] When asked why they bought a product, for example, respondents may reply in terms of a product characteristic, or they may explain that they just happened to see it on the shelf, or they may refer to a friend who had used it in the past. The interpretations are numerous.

Probably the most direct alternative to "Why" is to begin the question with the word "How."[16] "How did this happen or come about?" is less antagonistic and, therefore, more likely to elicit an informative response. If it is necessary to ask a "Why" question, never ask it in single word form. Tone it down by adding other words:

Why do you feel that way?

Why do you think that is so?

I wonder why you'd see it that way?

Why would you say that?

While the "why-type" question is the most obvious question to ask in order to get a respondent to elaborate, there are other effective and more subtle tricks of the trade. The most unobtrusive and neutral technique is silence (since it neither designates the area of discussion nor structures the answer in any way). Inexperienced interviewers have a difficult time in using the silent probe because they are overly concerned with maintaining a continuous flow of verbal interchange. The respondent is bombarded, caught in a hailstorm of questions—"Why is that important to you? How do you suppose such attitudes came about? Why? How many times? Why? Why?" Psychoanalysts have been very successful in using silent probes in therapy sessions. It conveys a relaxed mood and reinforces the notion that the researcher is not "imposing" anything on the respondent. It communicates: "Yes, I'm with you, go on," or "I'm waiting, sensing that you haven't finished," or "That's good, but what else do you think?"

Another elaboration technique widely used in psychotherapeutic counseling is the echo: an exact or nearly exact repetition of the respondent's words by the interviewer.[17] For instance, if a respondent were to offer the following "My experience on Amtrak was very upsetting," the interviewer may echo "You were very upset?" The echo, or "verbatim playback" does not exhibit the same intrusive qualities of a "Why?" It is an indirect way of saying "I am listening carefully and I want you to continue; to explain yourself in greater detail." It offers sympathy and encouragement while cueing the respondent to refocus his or her attention on the research question. The following is an illustration of the technique in a depth interview on toilet soap:

Q: What's the best toilet soap you've ever used?
A: Camay, definitely. I always use it when I go out in the evening.

Q: You always use it when you go out in the evening?
A: Well, I often go dancing . . . there are always masses of people there, but I feel more at ease if I've used it.[18]

A more difficult form of echoing is the paraphrase. This involves summarizing what the respondent has said in order to assist him or her in ex-

amining attitudes as a basis for self-insight. The interviewer is attempting
to function as a mirror for respondent's attitudes so that they can see themselves better. The use of analogies and metaphors are particularly useful in
capturing the respondent's emotions:

Q: Could you describe the factors that influenced your house buying?
A: Well, there were so many things . . . it was so confusing.

Q: Mm-hm.
A: Of course, price was the most important since this was our first house.
We didn't have that much money to put down. But we were also con-
cerned about location because of the school district the kids would be in.
We needed a good size yard, too.

Q: It sounds as though you had a rope tied around each arm and leg—
and being pulled in four different directions.
A: Yes! We also were concerned about the commute for my husband.
Several places we found were almost an hour away from his job.

The problem relative to clarification is somewhat more straightforward. It
is not a matter of attempting to figure out how to probe deeper or cover
new territory, we are simply trying to more fully define what territory has
already been covered:

Q: You mentioned you were part of the system. What did you mean by
that?

Q: Could you clarify something for me...?

Q: What did you mean when you said...?

How to Interrupt

While much of our earlier discussion dealt with techniques designed to encourage communications, there are times that the interviewer needs to
shorten or terminate a response so that they can probe in another direction.
The respondent could be (1) wandering off the topic, (2) covering ground
which was already covered or (3) going into a level of detail which is not

appropriate given the research question. One very effective, yet subtle, way of shortening responses is the discreet use of the "guggle."

> We became aware of the guggle while listening to large numbers of interviews. It occurs while the respondent is speaking and consists of short, usually staccato sounds made by the interviewer to indicate that he wants to say something. It often consists of "Ah" exclaimed singly, doubly and triply, but also may be the beginnings of words which are not completed. If the respondent ignores them, guggles often become increasingly frequent and eventually constitute a full interruption. Most interviewers are unaware that they use guggles, and there are wide individual differences among interviewers in the frequency with which they use them. Because the guggle puts the respondend on notice that the interviewer is eager to something, it may well have the effect of shortening responses. [19]

Unfortunately, at times the guggle is not sufficient to curtail some respondents' talkative nature. A more direct method occurs when the interviewer waits until the respondent finishes a sentence or thought, and then forcefully intercedes. The key, of course, is to put a halt to the discussed topic, but to avoid alienating the respondent. Several of the more subtle approaches might be:

> "We don't have a great deal of time, so perhaps we should move along."

> "Let's move to a related topic . . ."

> "I think we have enough on this. Now let's talk about . . ."

While a major goal of the interviewer is to encourage communication, the interviewer must not lose sight of the research objectives. And at times those research objectives require that the interviewer be as skilled at discouraging communication as at encouraging it.

COMMUNICATIONS FLOW

In obvious contrast to the group interview, the depth interview is a one-to-one interaction. The social system, consequently, is very simple, with the interviewee responding to the interviewer's questions and the interviewer reacting to the interviewee's answers. For the moment, it is appropriate to concentrate on the general role of the interviewer in the interviewing process just described. A major function that the interviewer performs is to increase the flow of relevant communications. Within this role, the interviewer can increase the flow of relevant information by employing various tactics to minimize the inhibitors and maximize the facilitators of communication. First, we will review six inhibitors.

Inhibitors[20]

The inhibitors categories discussed below act to prevent the communication flow. The first three tend to make the interviewee unwilling to give information, while the final three tend to make the respondent unable to give information even though willing.

Demands for Time. A depth interview may take anywhere from 15 minutes to several hours to complete. This is time the respondent could use to do other things and, therefore, the interview must compete against other activities. First, the interviewer must sell the idea of being interviewed in order to gain individual's initial cooperation. And while this may prove to be somewhat easy to do with individuals with flexible schedules, it may require innovative selling approaches with a busy executive. The interviewer should also be concerned with trying to get the respondent to "set aside" an appropriate amount of time so that interruptions or other pressing commitments do not interfere.

Ego Threat. Respondents may withhold information because of a psychological block due to the increased intimacy which is related to depth interviewing. For example, they may not admit to the use of some consumer products (e.g., perfume, clothing) in a sexual manner because they have actually convinced themselves that such thoughts do not reflect the attitudes of the Outer-Self. At other times, the respondent hesitates to communicate honestly because of fears of eliciting the disapproval of the interviewer. And finally, while the respondent may not be concerned with the interviewer, he or she may be fearful of public disclosure of their personal feelings. The interviewer can overcome many of these ego threats by (1) indirect questioning and probing, (2) expressing a sympathetic and nonjudgmental attitude, and (3) giving assurance of anonymity.

Culture. There is a set of "do's and don'ts" that are imposed on individuals via their particular environment. It has been noted, for example, that "It is accepted that there are things which men do not discuss in front of women and vice versa, things that married couples do not discuss in front of unmarried people, things students do not tell teachers, things doctors do not tell patients, things parishioners do not tell the clergy, etc."[21] Additionally, there is a desire to respond to questions within a range of cultural acceptance, avoiding any embarrassment, shock or threats. The best way to minimize this communication block is to "match" interviewer and interviewee. As much as possible, the interviewer should be an equal, with similar social class and background.

Forgetting. At times the respondent is unable to report relevant information because of an inability to recall it. In marketing and advertising we are continually asking people to reconstruct what they did or why they did it. Most people in an interview situation are trying to help, but their ability to give truthful answers are compromised by the passage of time since the event and the relative importance of the event. Time lapse is sometimes controllable by the interviewer; he or she should attempt to select respondents whose experiences are fresh. Another technique is to notify the interviewee in advance as to the nature of the interview, thus allowing them additional time to reconstruct the events.

Confusion by Influence. This is inaccuracy due to (1) faulty induction, when the respondent is asked to convert concrete experiences into a higher level of abstraction and (2) faulty deduction, when the respondent is asked to give specific examples of a general statement. Mistakes may result from the respondent's failure in abstract logic. The concrete experiences are not relevant to the generalization: while the facts may be correct, the conclusion is not. Also, the respondent may hold a very strong opinion concerning a generalized form of information such as "I really think the Boston Symphony caters to snobs," or "Breakfast cereals are for kids." All of these conclusions are value judgments that act as premises for any subsequent questions which require specific examples.

Unconscious Behavior. When using the depth interview technique we are often interested in probing attitudes. Some activities—such as using shampoo or choosing a wine—are repetitive behaviors and do not have clearly defined elaborations. They have become so ingrained that most people cannot articulate specific reasons. The interviewer must avoid prompting the respondent (for example, "Do you think you use this shampoo because you like the feeling of being clean all over?") and instead must use indirect questions and be willing to accept an "I don't know" answer.

Facilitators

While the interviewer should make every effort to overcome or minimize the communication inhibitors, attention should also be given to a set of "facilitators," the objective being to increase the flow of relevant information and create a situation which optimizes interpersonal relations. There are six major communication facilitators.

Establish Expectations. The interviewer must develop an environment in which it becomes apparent to the interviewee that cooperation is necessary. This entails the obvious verbal act of asking the respondent for cooperation but also the use of non-verbal communication which signals the interviewee that cooperation is expected. The most common way of establishing expectations is to convey an air of self-assurance. The interviewer gives off subtle cues (e.g., the way he or she sits, the gestures that are made) which signal the respondent. The key is to send signals that say "I know what I am doing," and "I expect you to go along with this."

Recognition. It must be remembered that the depth interview is a social interaction and, as such, there is a social exchange. The interview is a *quid pro quo* in which the interviewer receives information. But what does the respondent receive in return? Praise, approval and esteem are sources of ego gratification which should be conveyed to the respondent. All people need to feel appreciated, and experimental studies of interviewing have shown that praising the respondent's cooperation has a positive effect on the interview.[22] The skillful interviewer, therefore, should take every opportunity to recognize the importance of the respondent's contribution.

Altruistic Appeal. Another form of the social exchange goes beyond the personal need for recognition which is "inwardly" motivated. An altruistic appeal emphasizes that the time and effort that a respondent devotes to the interview will have an external reward. Academic researchers have an advantage in stressing the importance of basic research designed to enable them to better understand people and their environments. But practitioners are not without leverage. One approach is to stress the fact that "Company X is trying to understand your individual needs and wants in order to do a better job of satisfying all of its customers." The interviewee is portrayed as a spokesperson for an entire class of people.

Catharsis. Everyone needs to vent frustrations or, at the very best, they require a vehicle for expressing their opinions. An interview can provide this function by encouraging the respondent to verbalize hostility, guilt, frustration, hopes and fears. The interviewer, therefore, is providing a service much akin to that of a psychoanalyst when probing sensitive issues—it's almost a release:

> The interviewer simply slips into the informant's life and after an hour or two leaves it again. She does not argue or criticize, she makes no demands, she just listens. The informant is free to talk without any fear of the consequences; and it is surprising how much people will talk and what they will say when they get a chance.[23]

Sympathy. The most basic internal reward that a respondent can receive is the simple fact that someone is there to listen to them. Teenagers appreciate anyone who really tries to understand them. Older people often have problems that no one takes time to hear. More generally, we have become a nation of talkers rather than listeners. The interviewer who can convey the notion that he or she is really interested in understanding what the respondent (consumer) has to say, will go a long way in facilitating good communication.

External Rewards. While the *quid pro quo* is often enhanced by recognition, catharsis, altruistic appeals and sympathy, the exchange may also be promoted through more tangible rewards. Cash and small gifts can be used effectively to compensate individuals for their time. In most situations it is important to offer the reward as a "token of appreciation" rather than as remuneration for one's time. And research has shown that if a potential respondent can be convinced to accept the token, they will feel the psychological need to "help" in the interview.[24]

The inhibitors and facilitators are factors that impact the communication flow between the interviewer and respondent. And, therefore, it is reasonable to see a major role of the interviewer as being related to these factors—minimizing the negative forces and maximizing the positive ones.

DATA ANALYSIS

The issues of transcribing qualitative data and data reduction were discussed in the previous chapter. The statements that were made and the conclusions that were reached are equally applicable to depth interviewing data. It is appropriate, however, to extend the discussion a bit further. All interview data, whether group or depth, involves a compromise between opposing tensions. On the one hand there is the need to preserve the original detail of qualitative impressions. Earthy and rich commentaries are detailed within intricate contexts. On the other hand is the need to deal with the potentially overwhelming amount of information which, at times, appears to defy any attempt at systematic analysis.

Historically, social scientists who want to classify qualitative data into categories have used a process of classification known as "content analysis" or "coding." In his 1952 classic work on content analysis, Berelson defined the process as follows: "Content analysis is a research technique for the objective, systematic, and quantitative description of the manifest content of communication."[25]

The requirement that content analysis be objective requires us to proceed in our research with sufficient exactness such that other researchers would reach the same conclusions. Usually, this means strict attention to the definition of coding categories. As one researcher has commented:

> "When we listen to tapes from a focus interview, draw subjective impressions, and then perhaps reach consensus in discussions with others working on the study, we may be reaching conclusions that are more closely related to ourselves as receivers than to the content of the messages on the tape; in this case, we are not adequately fulfilling the requirements of objectivity."[26]

It is possible to have a sufficient amount of objectivity and yet have systematic bias. The usual manner in which such bias creeps into a coding scheme is when relevant categories are excluded. The result is a data reduction process which does not reflect the general body of information.

It is important, therefore, in any content analysis procedure to define categorical schemes which are mutually exclusive, totally exhaustive of the relevant content, and as precise as possible, so that coding becomes a clerical task rather than a judgmental one.

The final element is quantification. According to Kassarjian, quantification is the most distinctive feature of content analysis and argues that it "distinguishes content analysis from ordinary critical reading."[27] In most instances, the quantification process in content analysis is a matter of simply noting the presence or absence of a category within the collected qualitative data. This lowest level of measurement can be performed on words (e.g., the number of times the word "pretty" was mentioned), collection of words (e.g., a series of words which mean "pretty," such as "beautiful," and "attraction"), or themes (e.g., the number of times a negative comment was made).

While content analysis can be a rather stark distillation of impressionistic data into a list of words and numbers, the computer has enabled social scientists to get the best of both worlds—data reduction and qualitative detail. The most straightforward example of this is the use of word processing programs to do basic text analysis. Many software packages are available which will provide word counts, number of sentences, average sentence length, average word length, number of different key words, and several other features. A partial list of some of the more versatile software packages would include:

KWIX II	Skyline Software Falls Church, VA
Lazy Writer	AlphaBit Communication Dearborn, MI
Sensible Speller IV	Sensible Software Oak Park, MI
Ful/Text	Fulcrum Technologies Ottawa, Canada
CrystalWriter	Syntactics Santa Clara, CA

IRIS   Gallup & Robinson Inc.
                              Princeton, NJ

Verbatim Analyzer   Marketing Metrics
                              Paramus, NJ

It is easy to see how this might be useful. An image study or an advertising testing study would be interested in generating responses to an attitude object. The researcher could force subjects to respond to scale items; for example, a five-point scale from Interesting to Uninteresting. Or, the researcher could ask an open-ended question—"Could you tell me your reactions to this advertisement?" The word "interesting may be used by the subject to describe the ad, or the subject may use another word—perhaps the word "different." In fact, the word "different" may be mentioned 25 times over a series of 12 interviews, while "interesting" is not mentioned at all.

A second way in which computers can make content analysis useful to the researcher gathering qualitative data is through a "dictionary-driven" procedure. The grandfather of this procedure is the General Inquirer system developed by Stone et al. in 1962.[28] This system enables the researcher to quantify units of meaning by grouping words together which are related to that meaning. For example, one psychosociological dictionary classifies over 3500 words into fewer than 100 tags relevant to psychological or sociological analysis of text. A tag might be for the unit of meaning "danger," and would include such list words as "danger," "violence," "hit," "hitting," "kill," "killing," "smash," "fight," and "threat." Such dictionaries have been created for anthropological concerns and political science applications. According to Van Tubergen:

"Dictionaries of about 4000 words are usually adequate to recognize over 95% of the words in typical text and to assign correct meaning to these words about 95% of the time. Depending on the nature of your study, one of the existing dictionaries might be highly appropriate to your research; or perhaps it would be valuable to develop a dictionary for general use in market atttitude studies."[29]

Objectivity, quanitification and computers tend to convey the notion that counting is a rote process that results in page after page of sterile lists. But when we can identify a theme running through the data we are actually isolating something that is occuring more often. Our judgment of "a theme" is based upon counting; the observation is being made that one thing is occuring with greater frequency than something else. Given that content analysis or coding is merely a method of counting, the idea of counting words or synonyms can be expanded to counting *any* category that the researcher has defined or that emerges from the data. For example:

In a study into a client company's image we interviewed respondents from five major markets. Within each market we interviewed both employees and customers of our client's company. During the analysis of the interview-transcripts, and in line with some of our research questions, we coded any mention of 'qualities of the company' and 'qualities of their products.' These instances were further coded according to whether they were favorable or unfavorable comments. The results were then pooled together in a single matrix (only partial results listed below).

Market	Employees/ Customers	Company Qualities		Product Qualities	
		Pos.	*Neg.*	*Pos.*	*Neg.*
France	Employees	Reliable Competent Swedish	Low profile	Fast operation operation	
	Customers	Reliable	Low profile	Fast operation Reliable	
Germany	Employees	Reliable	Low profile	Innovative	
		Good ser- vicing	Confusion over name		
	Customers	Good technology	Low profile	Excellent products	
			Confusion over name		

As well as identifying the major qualities of the company and its products (both positive and negative), this matrix reveals certain patterns:

Company employees tended to concentrate on the positive qualities of their company whereas their customers were more likely to mention qualities of the products.

With the exception of Spain, there was universal agreement amongst both employees and customers in every market that the company had too low a profile.

With the exception of the company profile, a majority of respondents did not mention any negative qualities of either the company or its products; however, customers in both the UK and USA were critical of both the company and its products.

This last finding led us to carry out a number of further analyses in order to establish why these two markets were so different from the other European markets.[30]

The clustering of data is a method for counting and inferring something from the patterns that emerge. Content analysis can proceed from a strict counting of words to a broader categorizing procedure. Most recently the ability to collect narrative data in computer-readable form has led some researchers to pursue longer scale, qualitative studies which can ask the important "Why" questions in a cost effective manner. One methodology has been detailed by Becker and Nowak; an Everyday-Life-Approach to opinion and market research. Interviewers conduct depth interviews with individuals in order to explore lifestyles regarding a particular product—perhaps automobiles. The taped interviews along with various sociodemographic data are stored on magnetic disk. Becker and Nowak go on to comment:

"The printout of the conversation protocol is coded and analyzed by a scientifically trained staff member. 'Coding' means that the entire conversation is segmented according to content with a numerical code assigned to each text element. For example: the lines of an interview are consecutively numbered. From line 25 to line 48, the conversation partner talks about 'occupational stress.' This topic has the code number 010105, and the interview text is marked accordingly. The whole conversation is structured in this manner."[31]

Given this data bank, there are numerous possibilities for analyzing and presenting data. For example, an automobile manufacturer may want to know about the concerns of young single women and the mechanical maintenance of their automobiles. This demographic group can be easily retrieved. Then the corresponding parts of the text regarding mechanical maintenance are printed out. These parts of the text form the basis for further quantitative and qualitative content analysis. As can be seen, these advances in data analysis can fill a methodological gap between small group discussions, which may give impressionistic understanding but no statistical basis, and large quantitative surveys, which often produce pages of numbers with no depth of meaning.

TRADE-OFFS

As with obervation methods and group interviewing, each research technique has a set of characteristics that should be mentally reviewed each time a research design is developed. The depth interview is no different in that respect. While its strengths are significant, its weaknesses can, at times, be overwhelming.

Strengths

Individual Differences. The latitude of response patterns can be extremely different across individuals. In statistical terminology it simply means that many responses to questions can elicit what would amount to a large degree of variance. Although a mean (average response) can be calculated, a substantial percentage of the responses do not tightly congregate around that average. Instead a broad range, or dispersion, of attitudes occurs. Obviously, the wider the response pattern, or diversity of opinion, the less likely that a set of categories will be able to capture the differences. Since the unit of analysis in depth interviewing is the individual, it is extremely probable that the technique will be able to identify such idiosyncracies.

Unaided Recall. With most research techniques the respondent is cued; is asked, for instance, how important style or economy is when rating refrigerators. Or the respondent might be asked to rate two different political candidates on leadership and knowledge of the issues. All of these attributes (style, economy, leadership, knowledge) have been provided by the researcher. But often it is more important to see what a respondent will volunteer on a subject before specific prompting—finding out, perhaps, that 'style' wasn't even a relevant issue. By letting the subject generate the main points of discussion, there is a greater chance that those topics will reflect real concerns, rather than those imposed by the researcher.

Increased Validity. By validity we mean the extent to which we are able to observe, measure, or evaluate what is intended. The interview situation offers a unique opportunity to appraise the validity of self-reporting. Selltiz et al. have noted that "The interviewer is in a position to observe not only what the respondent says but also how he says it. He can, if he wishes, follow up contradictory statements. If need be, the interviewer can directly challenge the subject's report in order to see how consistent his answers will be."[32] The simple fact is that the interviewer has numerous options for approaching a topic. A question can be rephrased a number or different ways in order to ensure that the interviewee is consistent. One only needs to see a trial lawyer in action, relentlessly hammering at a particular point from many different angles, to see the advantage of an open-response format. This is not to insinuate that respondents are continually evading the truth but the depth interview can act in a very disarming fashion, resulting in respondents being amazingly direct and honest. For example, one researcher tells this "interviewing" story:

> A study among physicians about a category of prescription drugs asked why doctors didn't prescribe a certain drug. One reply: "It's too hard to spell." Suspicions confirmed.[33]

Clarification. In a questionnaire, if the subject misinterprets a question, doesn't understand a word, or records an answer in a confusing way, there is little that can be done to remedy the situation. In an interview, further questions can be asked, meanings clarified, and sentences rephrased. Confusion on a question or response is minimized. Increased flexibility also enables the researcher to play the role of a sleuth, deviating from a prepared script to investigate new avenues. "When the emphasis is upon discovery as opposed to measurement, we must give serendipity a chance to operate and allow the interviewer to pursue hunches and clues he may get as the interview progresses."[34]

Probing. As we have seen, the interview is an appropriate technique for revealing information about complex, emotionally laden subjects or for probing the sentiments that may underlie an expressed opinion. We know that human behavior is rarely, if ever, directly influenced or explained by an isolated variable. Many factors and conditional circumstances interact to create complexities that can only be unraveled when the researcher is able to probe individual responses. Not only are human attitudes and behaviors complex, they also can involve social posturing and simplifying. The "public" response is all too easy to give and may not reflect true differences. Kinsey, in his historic interviews on sexual behavior, developed an entire set of interviewing tactics that enabled him to overcome reluctance on the part of the respondent—"The interviewer should not make it easy for the subject to deny his participation in any form of sexual activity. It is too easy to say no if he is simply asked whether he has ever engaged in a particular activity."[35]

Weaknesses

The strengths of interviewing are significant and it is evident that its flexibility makes it adaptable to many research problems. In some situations, however, its advantages are not enough to compensate for its inherent weaknesses. In order to make the correct choice of technique(s), the limitations described below should be kept firmly in mind:

Individualization. By concentrating on differences the researcher is often left with a mass of individualized data that defies generalizations—"Because of the elaborate detail that can be apprehended by a good field worker, each situation or person is likely to be perceived as unique (as indeed they actually are). This uniqueness inhibits attempts at generalization and may inhibit the formulation of categories, types, and operational procedures for specifying variables the researcher is interested in."[36] The result is that any generalization that does occur is dependent upon the impressionistic interpretation of a large mass of data.

Expense. In terms of time and money there is no more expensive data-gathering technique available to consumer researchers. A half-dozen group sessions, hundreds of mail surveys and thousands of telephone interviews may be more time and cost efficient than 50 depth interviews. While this does not mean that the value of the information is any greater with such techniques, it merely reinforces the notion that the cost of employing depth interviews can easily be prohibitive. It also reinforces the fact that cost has to be weighed against the value of the resulting information. The fact that depth interviews are expensive should not automatically eliminate them as an option; those 50 depth interviews may, simply, provide better information than the one thousand telephone interviews.

Hired Hands. At times, many interviewers are hired—non-professionals who are told to go and "make conversation." The difficulty with this is twofold. First, different interviewers will interpret questions differently, will probe at different points, and will perceive responses in a different manner. This can result in a substantial degree of variability in the data, with no amount of training being able to negate totally the differences. If one attempts to deal with this difficulty by narrowly defining the permissable behavior of each interviewer, the "depth" interview can easily be reduced to a standardized question-and-answer session. Second, one researcher has enumerated a set of scenarios that can occur when the interviewer is not the researcher.[37] The least detrimental is a lack of attention to detail with the worst being outright lying, cheating and faking results.

Interviewer Bias. The effect that the interviewer has on the nature of the interviewee's responses has been the subject of extensive investigation across many disciplines. For example:

Hyman reported a study in which Negro and white interviewers each interviewed a random sample of Negroes on problems of discrimination. Negro interviewers obtained significantly more information on resentment over discrimination than did the white interviewers.[38]

A study by Ferber and Wales on opinions toward prefabricated houses showed that the respondents of interviewers who favored such housing themselves were more favorable to prefabricated houses than were respondents of interviewers who were unfavorable.[39]

Rice was struck by the fact that two interviewers reached such consistently different results in a study to determine causes of destitution, with the respondents being transients in flophouses. The men interviewed by one interviewer consistently cited overindulgence in liquor as the cause, whereas the respondents of the second interviewer tended to blame social and economic conditions. Later it was discovered that the first interviewer was a confirmed prohibitionist and the second a devoted socialist![40]

Respondent Bias. In the same respect, the respondent may alter his or her responses dependent upon the interviewer. For example, the background characteristics (age, education, socioeconomic status, race, religion, sex, and so on.) of the respondent will determine how they interface with the interviewer. If the respondent is in his teens, he may very well react differently to questions offered by a younger man than an older woman. He may be more helpful and truthful when identifying with one, more evasive and closed when speaking with the other. Such biases are also dependent upon psychological factors (perceptions, attitudes, expectations, motives) that the respondent brings to the interaction.

FINALITIES

Bedside Mannering

Much of the methodology regarding depth interviewing procedures have come from other disciplines. On the other hand, as we have seen, many of the techniques are appropriate regardless of the topic under investigation. For example, is diagnostic interviewing in the medical field that much different from the process of generating elaborations on how a consumer chooses a doctor, hospital, or health maintenance organization?

Q: Same kind of a pain you've had before over a past number of years?
A: That's right. I got up one day, I can't remember whether it was in the morning or the afternoon—but I felt it, you know what I mean, I felt it between here and here, and I guess—I think I got one or two just slight jabs like, you know, and I held on and kinda tried to get my air again, and I told my wife about it, or ex-wife, let's say, and I sat around for a while and the pain went away, and I went outside and it never bothered me after that and—

Q: This was when?
A: About three weeks ago.

Q: Well, is this the same time you talked about—you told me about last night, that came on all of a sudden?
A: No—no.

Q: It was before that.
A: That stopped until Monday morning about eight o'clock.

Q: Well, now talking about the time when it came on suddenly three weeks ago. You said you were working on a fence at that time?
A: Yes, I was. But I think I was in the house at the time. I remember because—

Q: In other words you weren't working on a fence at that time?
A: Well, I'd been working on the fence, I tell you the truth for— oh—two or three—

Q: Well, that's what I'm getting at—you weren't working on the fence when this happened?
A: No. No. I have been doing that for two, three months now and it's pretty hard pounding the nails, but I was in the house when this happened.

Q: You were in the house. Do you remember when you woke up that morning if you had a pain?
A: No, it didn't hurt me then.

Q. Well, how did it come on?
A. Just like you were going to jab—like a couple of days back, just a slight pain, and I got scared and I kinda hung onto it, and then I got another real slight one, you know—like—

Q: This is the one you're talking about three weeks ago?
A: That's right.[41]

Managerial Insights

Summon Your Strength. Depth interviewing is an exhausting experience if properly conducted. It is a game of psychological cat and mouse. It yields mounds of data which do not fit into nice, neat categories. The task should not be easy because nothing about it is easy. On the other hand, it is often the correct procedure to follow. The rewards are significant.

Target The Sample. Given that probability sampling is not possible with the depth interview, that does not mean that a sampling plan is not important. While convenience sampling may be appropriate at times, it is often more likely that very specific subjects should be included. One approach in this regard is known as the "key informant" technique. The key informant technique is a method of gathering information used by anthropologists who have used it extensively in their studies of the structure and behavior of cultures. Campbell explains the use of key informants:

> . . . the technique of the informant means that the social scientist obtains information about the group under study through a member who occupies such a role as to be well-informed but who at the same time speaks the social scientist's language. It is epitomized by the use of one or a few special persons who are extensively interviewed and upon whose responses exceptional reliance is placed.[42]

Given their role or status, key informants are not chosen randomly but on a selective basis. It is possible that quite a number of broad-based marketing studies using survey methods could be better designed as small depth interviewing studies targeting individuals with specialized knowledge.

Don't Divide By Eight. The typical size of a group interview is eight respondents. A mechanistic approach would say that during a one-hour group session every respondent could speak for seven or eight minutes. That, according to some, is a better investment since you can probe eight in the same time that you could one in a depth interview. In fact, a recent Advertising Research Foundation publication notes the following:

Amount of Information

Focus Group—A relatively large amount of information can be obtained in a short period of time with relatively small cost.

Depth Interview—A large amount of information can be obtained, but it takes time to do so and also to analyze the results. Thus costs are relatively high.[43]

This approach does not take into account the value of the information—one depth interview with a key informant has greater information value than a group session of eight uninformed respondents. Expected value is what is of importance, not the out-of-pocket expense.

Cases

The following represent a series of actual case histories in which the depth interview was used as an effective research tool:

1. Having reached a sales plateau, an industrial printing company was faced with what they thought were two different choices. One was to seek new customers; the other was to increase sales to existing customers. They quickly found out that the cost of identifying new customers (because the industry was so fragmented) was excessive. Instead, a series of depth interviews were held with the purchasing agents of their own customers. The interviews revealed that the decision process, needs, and manner of usage was very specific to the company—virtually no two customers were alike. The results of the research initiated a shift in company emphasis away from being "all things to all people" to nurturing a tighter, more symbiotic relationship between the printing supplier and printing user.

2. A smaller, regional, solar-unit manufacturer and distributor was interested in getting further information on the nature of "solar buyers'" reasons for buying. They knew that people who were buying were quite different from the general population (more wealthy, younger, higher education, suburban). They also knew that such innovators were important to their long-run success since they acted as opinion leaders. Depth interviews were held with the innovators and initial "reasons for buying" included economics, naturalness of the process, and intellectual curiosity. However, after probing on these responses, it was discovered that a very important reason was the social uniqueness of being the "first on the block." Additional depth interviews of people in the same neighborhood revealed that those who had considered solar equipment were concerned about reliability and economy. This information resulted in a two-pronged sales strategy. Sales presentations were changed depending upon whether the customer knew of someone in their neighborhood or circle of friends who

had purchased solar. If not, social uniqueness was subtly implied and if so, then reliability and economy were stressed.

3. A college president recently spent the summer traveling across the country interviewing national leaders in business, government, foundations and education. He discussed with them the challenges facing private higher education. After weeks of fact-finding and picking some of the finest brains on the various subjects, the president began to develop a feel for the major, common lessons which seemed to surface.

4. A bank was interested in increasing its sales of retirement planning products. Initial research efforts indicated that accountants were a key to product sales. They were advising their clients to consider the various retirement products in order to reduce their taxable income. In order to begin to understand such issues as the important attributes, knowledge level, fee sensitivity and other items, it was decided to generate information from the initiator—the accountants. A series of focus groups were scheduled. However, recruiting efforts were dramatically unsuccessful. It seemed that very few accountants wanted to discuss their beliefs or practices in public. Instead, depth interviews were used to explore privately the belief systems and behaviors of the accountants.

ENDNOTES

[1]Knos, Michele Z. (1986), "In-Depth Interviewing Can Reveal What's in a Name," *Marketing News*, 20 (January 3), p. 4.

[2]Oldfield, R.C. (1941), *The Psychology of the Interview,* (Methuen & Co. Ltd.: London), p. 6.

[3]Menninger, K., M. Mayman and P. Pruyse (1963), *The Vital Balance: The Life Process in Mental Health and Illness,* (New York: Viking Press).

[4]Riesman, D., and M. Benney (1956), *The Sociology of the Interview,* Midwestern Sociologist, 18, 3-15.

[5]Osgood, C. (1940), *Ingalik Material Culture*, (New Haven: Yale University Press).

[6]Huxley, Aldous (1932), *Brave New World*, (Harper and Row: New York), p. 5.

[7]Turkel, Studs (1972), *Working*, (Avon Books: New York), p. 2.

[8]Levy, Clifford V. (1981), "The Depth Interview," in *Handbook of Package Design Research,* Walter Stern (ed.), (John Wiley and Sons: New York), p. 156.

[9]Kahn, Robert L. and Charles F. Connell (1957), *The Dynamics of Interviewing*, (John Wiley and Sons: New York), p. 80.

[10]*Advertising Age*, April 4, 1983, p. 16.

[11]Bingham, Walter Van Dyke and Bruce Victor Moore (1959), *How to Interview*, (Harper & Brothers: New York), p. 16.

[12]McNemar, Quinn (1946), "Opinion-Attitude Methodology," *Psychology Bulletin*, XLVI, p. 317.

[13]Wigmore, J.H. (1940), *A Treatise on the Anglo-American System of Evidence in Trials at Common Law,* (Little, Brown, and Co.: Boston), p. 128.

[14]Berent, Paul H. (1966), "The Depth Interview," *Journal of Advertising Research*, vol. 6, No. 2, p. 33.

[15]Lazarfeld, Paul F. (1935), "The Art of Asking Why," *National Marketing Research*, Vol. 1, No. 1.

[16]Berent, op. cit., p. 32.

[17]Gilmore, Susan (1973), *The Counselor-In-Training,* (Meredith Corp.: New York), p. 248.

[18]Berent, op. cit. , p. 34.

[19]Richardson, Stephen A., Barbara Dohrenwend, and David Klein (1965), *Interviewing: Its Forms and Functions,* (Basic Books: New York), p. 205.

[20]Much of this section and the next is based on Gorden, Raymond L. (1969), *Interviewing: Strategy, Techniques, and Tactics,* (The Dorsey Press: Homewood, IL), pp. 70–95.

[21]Gorden, op. cit., p. 76.

[22]Field, Joan B. (1955), "The Effect of Praise in a Public Opinion Poll," *Public Opinion Quarterly,* pp. 85–90.

[23]Berent, op. cit., p. 39.

[24]Hansen, R.A. (1980), "A Self-Perception Interpretation of the Effect of Monetary and Nonmonetary Incentives on Mail Survey Respondent Behavior," *Journal of Marketing Research*, February, pp. 77–83.

[25]Berelson, B. (1952), *Content Analysis*, (Free Press: Glencoe, IL).

[26]Van Tubergen, G. Norman (1978), "The Computer and the Content Analysis of Qualitative Response: Some Possibilities," in *Association for Consumer Research Proceedings,* John Eighmey (ed.), Chicago, IL.

[27]Kassarjian, Harold (1977), "Content Analysis in Consumer Research," *Journal of Consumer Research*, 4, June, p. 8.

[28]Stone, P. J., D. C. Dunphy, M. S. Smith, and D. M. Ogilvie (1966), *The General Inquirer: A Computer Approach to Content Analysis,* (Cambridgde: MIT Press).

[29]Van Tubergen, op. cit.

[30]Griggs, Steve (1987), "Analyzing Qualitative Data," *Journal of the Market Research Society*, 29, (January), p. 23.

[31]Becker, Ulrich and Horst Nowak (1983), "The Everyday-Life-Approach as a New Research Perspective in Opinion and Marketing Research," *European Research*, January, 20-29.

[32]Selltiz, Claire, Marie Jahoda, Morton Deutsch, and Start W. Cook (1951), *Research Methods in Social Relations*, (Henry Holt & Co.: New York), p. 242.

[33]Pope, Jeffrey L. (1981), *Practical Marketing Research*, (AMACOM: New York), p. 275.

[34]Gorden, op cit., p. 53.

[35]Kinsey, Alfred C., W.B. Pomeroy and C.E. Martin (1948), *Sexual Behavior in the Human Male,* (W.B. Saunders: Philadelphia), p. 53.

[36]Doby, John T. (ed.) (1954), *An Introduction to Social Research,* (The Stackpole Company: Harrisburg, PA), p. 226.

[37]Roth, Julius A. (1965), "Hired Hand Research," *The American Sociologist,* (November), pp. 190–196.

[38]Hyman, Herbert et al. (1954), *Interviewing for Social Research,* (University of Chicago Press: Chicago).

[39]Ferber, Robert and Hugh Wales (1952), "Detection and Correction of Interviewer Bias," *Public Opinion Quarterly*, 16, pp. 107-127.

[40]Rice, S.A. (1929), "Contagious Bias in the Interview: A Methodological Note," *American Journal of Sociology,* 35, pp. 420-423.

[41]Kahn and Connell, op. cit.

[42]Campbell, Donald T. (1955), "The Informant in Quantitative Research," *The American Journal of Sociology*, 60, p. 339.

[43]*Focus Groups: Issues and Approaches,* (1985), (Advertising Research Foundation: New York), p. 5.

CHAPTER SIX

PROJECTIVE METHODS

Ever since Ernest Dichter introduced techniques borrowed from the psychoanalytic school into the commercial world in the 1950s, consumer researchers have been intrigued by the potential of these methods. As with other clinical psychology methods, the approaches have an uncanny knack for peeling away the different layers of the human personality. The underlying belief system, the basic motivations that drive attitude formation and subsequent behavior, can be exposed to the researcher with the careful application of these methods. And such basic motivations exist in everyone, regardless of socioeconomic type, personality type, sex, *or even age.*

A national paper product manufacturer was seeking to develop a new concept—a cross between a bib and napkin for kids aged three to six. The advertiser wanted to find out if families needed this product and, if so, how children would use it. Children were given stuffed animals, dolls, and construction materials to use as they saw fit in the play tasks before them. Then the kids were placed into "pretend family-meal" scenarios and instructed to be parents and make the dolls and stuffed animals into their children. The youthful respondents soon seated their "pretend children" at make-believe dinner tables, trussed them up with a variety of bibs and napkins, and gave them long lectures on keeping clean at meals. The children also provided projective dialogue for their "pretend children," who liked to be messy and, accordingly, rejected certain kinds of bibs/napkins while approving others.

These sessions produced a lot of specific marketing data. Even though children wanted their chests covered by something that would protect their clothes, they did not like bibs tied around the neck because they felt "itchy and babyish." Instead, children wanted to be grown up and keep something on their laps. Eventually, a prototype product was developed on the basis of what was learned about childrens' needs and uses of bibs/napkins in these projective play sessions.[1]

Because of the uncertainty involved in the ability or desire of individuals to explain their motivations, it is reasonable to think that the most successful techniques aimed at uncovering motivations are of a qualitative variety.

People have a multitude of of reasons, many of them quite valid, for not wishing to divulge their inner feelings and thoughts to others. Fear of offending others, fear of retaliation from others, fear of embarassment or appearing foolish, silly, or stupid may also be involved. The wish to remain private, personal freedom and control, and self-dignity are other considerations. Moreover, in many situations an individual may be unable to recognize, recall, or describe accurately the nature of inner processes (certainly true in our above example).

Motivation research using projective methods is essentially diagnostic as opposed to descriptive. We are more interested in why something happened than in who did what. In marketing and advertising, therefore, the "motivation researcher" looks for the rational or irrational urges, drives, predispositions, hopes, prejudices and fears that cause people to act as they do toward the product, service, or situation. The emphasis is on understanding the basic determinants of behavior. As an example:

Do you know that some people think of their cars as masculine, whereas others think of their cars as feminine? That your product may offend by being underpriced? That the name of a high quality vitamin preparation made people think of motor oil? That an excellent product for the home was well liked by its buyers, but was seldom bought a second time because of too little snob appeal? Users liked it, but they were afraid of what their friends would think.[2]

The key difference between projective methods and group and depth interviewing, is that in order to probe beneath explanations and opinions the researcher needs to adopt an indirect approach. "Snob appeal" is not something readily admitted to and, consequently, admittance to this level of the Inner-Self must be disguised. Several definitions of these indirect, disguished techniques from non-marketing or advertising fields may prove useful:

In contrast with psychometric tests are those designed so that the variability of response between persons is great. The stimuli are usually ambiguous and permit each subject to interpret or structure it in his own way, thus evoking personality characteristics that are somewhat unique to him.[3]

Projective techniques are distinguished from other methods of assessment by the use of unstructured tasks and ambiguous materials. The examinee is given a minimum of instruction, and within the limits of the testing situation and the kind of material, he is free to go in his own directions and to give his own unique responses. It is hoped thus to obtain information concerning his personality by the fact that he projects himself into his responses.[4]

A projective technique is an instrument that is considered especially sensitive to covert or unconscious aspects of behavior, it permits or encourages a wide variety of subject responses, is highly multidimensional, and it evokes unusually rich or profuse response data with a minimum of subject awareness concerning the purpose of the test. Further, it is very often true that the stimulus material presented by the projective test is ambiguous, interpreters of the test depend upon holistic analysis, the test evokes fantasy responses, and there are no correct or incorrect responses to the test.[5]

Since the history of projective techniques is rooted in clinical psychology, these definitions may not prove to be particularly insightful, especially in terms of marketing or advertising. Fortunately, a classic marketing study is available to describe the ability of motivation research to induce an individual to talk about him or herself in a disguised form. Almost 30 years ago, Mason Haire tried to discover what factors determined the attitudes of housewives toward instant coffee.[6] Subjects were asked, "Do you use instant coffee?" [If no,] "What do you dislike about it?" Most of the unfavorable responses fell into the general area of "I don't like the flavor." Because this was a simple answer to a complex question, however, Haire suspected that it was a stereotyped response designed simply to answer the question and get rid of the interviewer.

The projective test which he developed to uncover any underlying motives consisted of two shopping lists of such items as "2 pounds of potatoes, 2 loaves of Wonder bread," and so on. The two lists were identical with the exception that one list contained "one pound Maxwell House coffee (drip grind)," and the other, "Nescafe instant coffee." Subjects were asked to read one or the other shopping list and characterize the woman who purchased these particular groceries. The woman buying the instant coffee was described as lazy, failing to plan schedules, not a good wife and not thrifty. The Maxwell House purchaser, in contrast, was described as thrifty, a good wife, not lazy, and a good planner.

The purpose of motivation methods, then, is to provide a means to increase the validity of research concerning peoples' motivations by disguising the purpose of the research. By getting people to talk about themselves in this way, they may disclose information that they could not or would not normally reveal. As such, the technique is much like a blood pressure cuff which is attached to your arm. It reveals something about yourself which you as a respondent could not express. In the same manner, the housewives in Haire's study "revealed" a relationship between instant coffee and the role of a housewife—a motivation that was not disclosed in the direct questioning in which taste emerged as the critical variable.

A HISTORICAL PERSPECTIVE

While the term "projective technique" was coined in the early part of this century, the concept of projection and motivation research has been implicitly used for centuries. Piotrowski points out that both Botticelli and Leonardo da Vinci alluded specifically to the usefulness of ambiguous stimuli in studying the process of creativity during the fifteenth century.[7] It is known that da Vinci used ambiguous stimuli as one of his techniques for selecting pupils by presenting them with a stimulus and observing the imagination and talent with which they struggled to generate artistic forms from it.

The nature of projection became more crystallized toward the end of the nineteenth century in the writings of Freud. In his early theory of motivation he proposed that the unconscious was largely made up of motives which were unexpressed and not accessible by simple questioning.[8] In attempting to diagnose and treat patients suffering from emotional disorders he noticed that these unconscious motivations were, at times, externalized. Specifically, patients had a tendency to ascribe their own drives, feelings, and emotions to other people or to the outside world in such a manner as to defend themselves. In succeeding years this narrow view of projection was significantly broadened. In fact, Freud (1911) wrote concerning projection that " . . . it makes its appearance not only in paranoia but under other psychological conditions as well, in fact it has a regular share assigned to it in our attitude to the external world."[9] By the 1930s the use of ambiguous stimuli had become a viable, although controversial, means of eliciting psychological assessments. The Rorschach test and the Thematic Apperception Test were both being used, and the term "projection" was popularized by Frank in a classic paper elaborating the "projective hypothesis" and offering the label "projective methods" for a variety of techniques useful to the clinician.[10]

As we have seen, it is generally agreed that our attitudes, motivations and emotions do not occur along one simple level. Instead, there seems to be an Outer-Self which we show to the world. This outer level is free and open to inquiry. Then there is at least one conscious inner level of personality, a level of wishful thinking and emotional drives which are disguised to the outer world by rationalizations and intellectualizations. And finally, there is a subconscious level, the Inner-Self, where are located the strong forces which the individual himself may not recognize— the basic drives of his unconscious mind. Given such a distinction between the public and the private, the worth of projective techniques become readily apparent. A frontal approach using various direct measurement methods will usually yield simplifications. The researcher needs to use different methods to penetrate into the inner levels of the individual in order to understand the private self.

Observation methods and group interviewing are useful at the outer levels; depth interviewing at a more subconscious level; projective methods are most useful for generating information at the most repressed level. Such projective methods are necessary because they enable the researcher to begin to understand the basic motivations underlying attitudes and behaviors. For example:

Men project some part of themselves into everything they do. Watch a man walk. Watch him drive a car. Listen to a woman talk to her husband. Examine an artist's paintings. Study a professor's lecture style. Observe a child play with other children, or with toys and dolls. In all these ways human beings express their needs, their drives, their styles of life.[11]

The advantage of such an "indirect" method of assessment is that it conceals from the individual the intent of the questioning. In the Haire study the role of women was assessed by manipulating a shopping list. The attitude object, in that case the instant coffee, was the source of a series of projections concerning the role of women in society, a role that had not been readily accessible through direct questioning. Thus, the way in which an individual projects him or herself into a task, situation, or object is a useful source of information for the psychologist or for that matter, the sociologist, the anthropologist—or the consumer researcher.

Given the acceptance of projective methods within the area of clinical psychology, it was only reasonable to expect that other social sciences would also put the procedure to the test. In the late 1940s, motivation research based upon the techniques of individual psychotherapy began to gain popularity as a way of eliciting consumers' true buying motives— why people buy or do not buy particular products and services. The difficulty in consumer research has always been that people give simplistic or evasive answers to questions, especially to "Why" questions: "Why do you use this brand?" . . . "Because I always buy it." or "Because it seems to work OK." Of course clinical psychologists have long been faced with a parallel set of problems: patients unable or unwilling to tell therapists what they think or how they feel. In marketing and advertising, then, we would like to know how people view promotional efforts, how product needs arise and grow until buying actions are initiated, and what determines brand selection once a decision is initiated. We need knowledge about the psychological and sociological determinants of consumers' behaviors.

The arrival of motivation researchers on the scene held great promise for marketing and indeed became the research craze of the 1950s and 1960s. While the "projective technique" fad has been supplanted by the "focus group" fad, the techniques of motivation research deserve close consideration in today's highly competitive and fragmented environment. Projective methods have limited but practical application as is evidenced by these classic examples:

John H. Breck, Inc. studied the feelings of women about the color of their hair. It found that women think of the color of their hair as a great and living personal symbol—an integral part of their personality. It was then able to assure women that Breck shampoo would only highlight the natural color of their hair. The ad appeal came closer to how women really feel.

The Miles Laboratories, Inc. found that its stingless antiseptic Bactine was too bland. Motivation researcher discovered that the mother who administered the cure without any sting, never got any part of the credit—no chance to comfort the child. So, part of the sting was put back.[12]

APPLIED TECHNIQUES

While the clinical psychology literature is replete with numerous projective methods (and variations), this section will not be an exhaustive description of those methods. Rather, our scope will be limited to those techniques which have proven to be useful in the analysis of current marketing and advertising problems. We can divide such applied techniques into four categories: association, construction, completion, and expression.[13]

Association

Philosophers through the ages have been aware of the association of ideas, the linking of words together to express thoughts. The "word association method," sometimes called the free association method, dating back to the 1880s, is perhaps the oldest procedure used in clinical psychology. The general approach is to read respondents a list of words (stimuli) and have them respond with the first words that come to mind. Such "associations" reveal the respondents' strongest attitudes toward the various stimuli.

The instructions that are used to generate these associations are fairly standardized: "I will read a list of words [or show you various symbols], one at a time, and I want you to tell me the very next word you think of. Any word is alright—the main thing is speed. For example, if I said 'college,' you might say 'education.' Do you understand?" The list of words or symbols contains both items of interest as well as neutral items. The purpose of the neutral items is to conceal the purpose of the study from the respondent in order to eliminate any response bias. In addition, the list is randomized in its order of items. The respondents, therefore, are simply responding to a list of items with the very first thought which they connect with the stimuli. The emphasis is on immediacy, with reflection, reason, or rationalization being minimized.

The uses of word association in marketing and advertising are extensive. For example, in naming a new product this method can be used to make sure that the name has the correct connotations. As an illustration, a liquor

manufacturer attempted to market a light whiskey and tested the names of
Verve, Ultra, Master's Choice and Frost. "Verve" was "too modern,"
"Ultra" was "too common," and "Master's Choice" was "not upbeat
enough." "Frost," however, was seen as upbeat, modern and clean—an appropriate image for their product.[14] Similarly, Smith reported a classic
study in which the stimulus words were Doeskin and Kleenex.[15] The
former drew a decidedly larger number of replies such as "soft," "softness," and "downy," suggesting the concept of softness is built into the
Doeskin brand name—an important feature in selling cleansing tissue.
Word association has also aided decision makers in naming museum exhibits, television shows and in changing the names of banks.
A second use is in the area of "brand personality." In order to establish
how people feel about a brand, word association can be used to enumerate
the human characteristics that people link to the brand. A recent example:

> It's hardly the sort of advertisement you would expect for an estab-
> lished mass-marketed brand like Maxwell House. Three young
> sophisticates sit around a cozy, candle-lit dinner table, reminiscing
> about old boyfriends and sipping different blends of coffee. "My
> fifth boyfriend my junior year. He was a number," recalls the woman
> drinking "indulgent" Kenya AA blend. "Odd. But interesting," adds
> the one tasting "beguiling" Special Reserve. And the third woman,
> who is having the "confident" Rich Dark Roast, remarks that,
> "Grown men don't wear saddle shoes."[16]

Since consumers may have trouble describing and assigning personality
characteristics, the immediate responses to a list of brands can be very enlightening. For example, Ralston Purina got the idea for shaping a new
personality for Ry Krisp because a word association study showed that
many people who did not use Ry Krisp seemed to associate it with diet-
ing.[17]
Another use is related to the need to identify the pivotal attributes of a
product or brand in order to direct the development of the advertising or
product research. Gilette's Dry Look was in response to research which
showed a positive association between "good grooming" and a "non-
greasy" look. Coincidentally, the dry look came twenty years after the
same methodology was used to move a product away from the "dry"
image:

Goetz beer in St. Louis, because of a motivation research job, switched its advertising against a trend. Other beers were being advertised as dry. The research showed the people don't associate beer with dryness; people drink it to quench their thirst. The ad slogan for Goetz was switched to "Wet and Wonderful." The package design was changed to show some cool ice skaters.[18]

During a "usual" word association procedure the respondent is presented with a list of words and asked to react to each with the first word that comes to mind. Successive-word association requires the respondent to continue to give single-word associations to the same test word for as long as he or she can. As such, successive-word association can enumerate the entire array of a subject's interpretive field and can be quite useful in the initial stages of questionnaire design. For example, the words "political candidate" could evoke "legislator," "honesty," "integrity," "leader," and so forth. In a political poll, such associations would be useful to a researcher choosing adjectives to use in the development of a set of attitude scales.

Free associations need not be limited to a word test. Indeed, a researcher could decide to elicit associations by showing an actual product, or set of pictures. Advertisers can expose consumers to advertising copy and layout. Individuals can be asked to give single-word or successive-word responses to headlines, logos, taglines, or pictures.

Finally, it should also be mentioned that there are situations where "free" association may not be possible or desirable. "Controlled" associations, by contrast, define the response set thereby limiting the respondent to certain classes of answers. While the controlled association method obviously cuts down the variety of responses, it has value in getting clear-cut answers to problems that are, in turn, limited in scope. For instance, one recent bank study was done in order to generate consumer feedback on a cross-sell program (i.e., using point-of-sales aids to simplify the account-opening procedure and to expose customers to additional services). The following instructions were read over the telephone to individuals who had previously opened accounts:

Take a moment and think back to that time several weeks ago when you walked into the bank to open the account. Picture in your mind what it was like. Pretend for a moment that you're actually sitting in the chair with the customer service representative. [pause] Now, I'm going to read you a list of adjectives and I would like you to tell me whether they describe your account-opening experience. A "Yes" means it does describe it and a "No" means it does not. Don't think too much about each one . . . we're interested in your first reaction. Now again, picture yourself sitting in the chair . . . [pause] . . . and here are the adjectives.[19]

The interviewer then proceeded to read through a list of 30 adjectives (e.g., relaxed, complicated, dull, pressured) with the respondent answering "Yes," "No," or "Not Sure."

Word association responses can be analyzed in several different ways. The most obvious method of analysis is to measure the frequency of various responses. In the previous study, for example, 11.1 percent of the respondents found the account-opening experience to be "Complicated," while 14.9 percent thought that it was "Dull." When a "free association" approach is used, a strict frequency count is usually replaced with an analysis of the patterns of content. Responses can be grouped so as to identify themes that represent concerns, motivations, interests, and beliefs. As such, it is reasonable to categorize associations as positive-negative, pleasant-unpleasant, flexible-inflexible, masculine-feminine, depending upon the problem. For instance, in a study of the image of a particular university, high school seniors could give a wide range of responses. Many of the responses would, however, fall into categories concerning the quality of university programs (good-bad), physical features (pleasant-unpleasant), athletics (strong-weak), and so on. The same would be true when attempting to reposition a consumer product or develop a public relations campaign for city.

The amount of time between the presentation of the test word and a response may also be useful as another form of of analysis. Usually people respond in less than 3 seconds but it has been noted that the length of delay may provide additional information: "Clinically, a long delay before responding to a given word may mean that some 'complex' has been tapped. In the consumer field, delay may indicate embarrassment or unconscious emotional involvement."[20]

And finally, it is possible that this form of motivation research can prompt overt behaviors which reflect internal emotions. Giggling, coughing, various hand gestures, looking away, facial changes, and so on illustrate the type of observations which can yield further explanatory data.

Construction

Another series of motivation techniques revolve around the ability of an individual to construct a story or dialogue in response to a stimulus. The stimulus is usually a picture but can also be a written narrative. In keeping with a basic premise of projection, it is necessary that the stimulus, whether pictorial or narrative, be ambiguous: "The theory behind the technique is that when stories are constructed around ambiguous pictorial (narrative) stimuli, the individual organizes the material around his personal experiences, his hopes and aspirations, and his conscious and semi-conscious need system."[21]

The current construction techniques that are used in marketing and advertising research are based upon a clinical procedure, the Thematic Apperception Test, which was developed for personality exploration by clinical psychology researchers. While the Thematic Apperception Test is a very structured procedure involving a series of 30 pictures with a scoring and interpretation scheme, the technique has been broadened and adapted for purposes of consumer research. A photograph, cartoon, or advertising layout can be used as stimuli in which specific marketing variables are imbedded. Attitudes toward products or product classes can be generated and the image of a company or industry can be explored. Factors that effect purchase behaviors, such as pricing considerations and options, can be learned—the entire purchase process can be exposed. In addition, since these techniques are generally conducted orally, probing questions can be used to obtain a comprehensive response to the marketing situation presented. Several examples can be used to illustrate this type of research:

A picture of a person with a quizzical look sitting at a personal computer could be used to explore the kinds of concerns which people have *after* a computer purchase.

A drawing of a consumer looking at a pair of sunglasses in a store. The fact that the individual is checking the price tag on the glasses would be used to evoke attitudes toward price sensitivity.

A photograph of a young person and his or her parents walking under an ivy-covered arch with the words "The University of Rhode Island" could be a useful approach in assessing the image of the institution.

Once a respondent is given a picture, the researcher would give instructions such as "Now make up a story about who this person is [these persons are] and what's going on. Any kind of story will do." In addition to these instructions an entire set of probes are appropriate—"What events led up to the scene in this picture?," "How do you feel about what they are doing?," "What is the person thinking?," "Why?," "What's going to be the outcome?"

It is possible, of course, to have respondents construct a story from a written narrative which describes a situation. The written narrative would require the respondents to make various observations or conclusions. As an example, if the manufacturer of industrial machinery was interested in the key factors that influenced purchase behavior, the following narrative might be presented to purchasing agents, operators, or executives:

The National Printing Press Convention was recently held in St. Louis, Missouri. As usual, manufacturers and users from across the country descended on the Convention in order to swap information and explore the most recent "happenings." On the floor of the Convention is a booth which houses one of the major manufacturers. Around a new press device are standing several representatives from the manufacturer, Ensign Printing Corporation, as well as three or four potential buyers. Their conversation is very animated.

The researcher would then probe for details of the conversation in order to elicit from the respondents a complete construction of the factors that influence a purchase decision or specifics concerning the image of Ensign Printing Corporation.

And finally, it is also appropriate at times to develop a research design which requires respondents to construct a picture-response. Imbedded in such picture-responses, or psycho-drawings, can be many attitudes or beliefs which are not easily expressed by the individual. Also, in some research situations a visual response provides a more accurate medium of expression than a verbal response. One vintage example is the construction approach used by Krugman to obtain the stereotyped perceptions of supermarkets by housewives.[22] A group of 50 New York housewives were given a pencil and a sheet of paper with a scaled outline of a supermarket on it. They were then asked to "draw a supermarket" with the location, names, and sizes of the various departments. the analysis of the picture-responses was based upon three aspects: "(1) store departments omitted, (2) order in which departments were drawn, (3) space allotted to each department."

As with most projective techniques, a construction approach is only limited by the imagination of the researcher. The stimulus can be most anything as long as it encompasses the research problem and is sufficiently ambiguous to allow the respondent to interpret the stimulus from a broad perspective. The response form is equally unstructured, with the key emphasis being on encouraging the respondent to combine his or her impressions into narrative or picture.

Completion

Completion techniques require that respondents react to ambiguous *and incomplete stimuli*. The most common method is "sentence completion," which asks respondents to complete a statement such as, "People who don't have savings accounts are . . ." While the stimulus can be a sentence, a story, or a picture, the common element is that the stimulus is not the entire scenario, it is not a complete thought. As such, completion techniques are different from construction methods in which the respondent reacts to a complete stimulus—a full story or a total picture. The respondents are offered only an initial portion of the stimulus; thus, they are free to use imagination and experiences to interpret the first part and then to take a position or express an attitude on how to complete the thought. In contrast to association methods, completion techniques allow the researcher to provide greater context for expressing the issue of concern. The respondents have more freedom in their reactions to the stimuli and, consequently, develop more extensive answers and more information.

As with other projective methods, the researcher should be aware of several options which can increase the effectiveness of various completion techniques. Because of the increased ability to target specific problems, completion techniques must be tempered by additional concerns for indirectness. For example, if a research problem is related to a sensitive issue such as personal financial matters, a frontal attack on the individual may cause lying or evasiveness. A question such as "I always have a difficult time choosing between saving money or spending it when . . ." may be better phrased as it was in the previous paragraph: "People who don't have savings accounts are . . ." Such third-person sentences are more "projective" in nature because in talking about others, respondents may be more willing to reveal a portion of themselves. Since the two types of sentences establish very different frames of reference for the respondents, the decision to use first-person or third-person should be carefully considered.

It is also necessary to consider the use of various neutral stimuli in order to disguise the specific intent of the research. In our banking example, it may be appropriate to include stimuli concerning consumer purchases in order to broaden the tone of the research; for instance, "People who purchase home satellite-dishes are . . ." Repeated attempts to focus narrowly on a sensitive issue may result in evasive answers which nullify the benefits of projective techniques.

Three basic completion approaches have been used in consumer research—sentence, story, and picture completion. Suppose one is interested in consumers' perceptions of gas as compared to oil heat. One might compose such incomplete sentences as: "A family which chooses to build a house with oil heat . . .," "The economic efficiency of gas heat . . .," "Keeping a house heated with gas heat . . ." Numerous different perspectives can be explored. In addition, sentence completion can be used to probe most research topics:

"The ads in *The New Yorker* . . ."

"Women who use a microwave oven to cook . . ."

"I like to smoke Merit cigarettes because . . ."

"Most insurance companies . . ."

In addition to sentence completion, more context and detail can be accumulated by using a story completion approach. The respondents are given the beginning of a story and asked to complete it. For instance, a U.S. import/export company was recently interested in importing a line of gourmet food and beverage products from Israel.[23] To date, most Israeli food products have been "kosher" and narrowly targeted to Jewish communities in the United States. The difficulty would be in probing the reaction of Midwesterners and Southerners to the idea of gourmet foods and beverages from Israel. Story completions could be developed around gourmet imports—French wines, Swiss Chocolates and such—one or more of which is from Israel. The story could proceed to describe a couple entering a small market specializing in international foods, choosing a few items and then picking up a specific product (that just so happens is imported from Israel). The respondents would then be asked to complete the story and, it is hoped, in the process reveal preferences, attitudes, anxieties, and concerns.

Finally, in the picture completion technique the respondent is shown an illustration which may be interpreted in several different ways. The picture is usually drawn as a cartoon showing two people without facial expressions or other characteristics (stick figures are often used) that would indicate socioeconomic background or a particular personality. This neutrality helps the respondents to identify with the cartoon characters. Advertisements, photographs, or other pictorial materials can also be used. In consumer research, the picture response usually employs illustrations of situations involving the use of a product or service. But as one researcher has noted, "The pictures can be modified to fit most kinds of marketing problems, ranging from image and preference studies to basic underlying consumer attitudes."[24]

The general picture completion scenario has characters making a "thought-provoking" statement in a speech balloon. The other person also has a speech balloon overhead, but it is conspicuously empty. The respondent is asked to complete the scene by filling in the second balloon. It is hoped, of course, that the respondents will project their own attitudes and beliefs into the role of the second character. For example, one picture completion task may show two men seated at a table having coffee. The first man says "I have been debating whether to buy a new car but I'm concerned about the resale value." The empty balloon attached to the second man should provoke a specific reaction from the respondent concerning the importance of resale value in the purchase decision. In another scenario, two businessmen are standing in a cocktail lounge having a drink, one is saying "I was wondering whether Providence Bank or Newbold Trust would be a better place to get that line of credit I need." The second businessman would be offering a general impression of the image of the two banks regarding commercial loans.

In constructing a picture completion task several key factors should be kept in mind. First, it is essential that the picture situation be relevant to the respondent. For example, a picture developed for a study showed a customer returning an item to a store. The picture completion task had to be abandoned, however, because most men could not identify with the situation.[25] And second, while it was noted that extraneous details can influence the neutrality of the setting, it is possible to make the picture scenario so "lifeless" as to render it unrealistic. There must be enough direction and vitality to the situation to focus the respondents' attention and entice them to become actively involved.

Expression

Expressive techniques are not dissimilar to construction techniques in that the respondent is required to produce or construct something—usually a story, or on occasion, a picture. But the emphasis with expressive techniques is on the manner in which construction occurs. The end product, or what is constructed, is less important than the process of activity. According to Kerlinger, "The subject expresses his needs, desires, emotions, and motives through working with, manipulating, and interacting with materials, including other people, in a manner or style that uniquely expresses his personality."[26] For example, asking an individual, who as part of his job buys electric motors, to assume the role of a salesman for New England Electric Motor Company, would put that individual in the position of expressing their opinions about the product. The attributes that are cited and the features that are avoided all give clues as to the opinions held by the respondent.

Several different expressive techniques have been successfully used in marketing and advertising research: role playing, personification, and play techniques. In role playing, respondents become actors by putting themselves in the place of other people; for example, "Imagine you are the President of Apple Computer Company . . . " While this may appear to be a highly artificial situation, it is something that we as individuals often do when we ask ourselves such questions as: "I wonder how she feels about me?", "I wonder how they ever reached that conclusion?" The playing of roles is a natural phenomenon for most people: "Sometimes we tend to play the role of the other person. We put ourselves in his place imaginatively and try to figure out how he feels on the basis of how we think we would feel under the same circumstances."[27]

Researchers have capitalized on this tendency to project one's own feelings into another person's situation by formalizing the process of role playing. Recently, one research project was conducted in order to understand rate sensitivity by electrical utility customers. The following task was given to a sample of those customers:

> You are on the editorial staff of the local newspaper. Your publisher has decided its time the newspaper took a position on the issue of rising electricity rates. He/she wants to write an editorial and has asked you to provide advice on the following issues.
>
> How would you describe electricity rates? Are they reasonable, unfair, excessively high, high but not Eastern Electric's fault, or what?
>
> What reasons do you give the paper's readers to support this?
>
> Should the editorial condemn the electric utilities or take a more moderate stand?[28]

Several key factors should be kept in mind when designing and conducting a role-playing exercise.[29] First, the respondent must be able to understand the extent of the part he or she is expected to play. The instructions, therefore, need to be the proper mixture of generality and specificity. Instructions such as "Play a consumer" may result in the respondent wandering too far from the topic under investigation. Much of the resulting information, therefore, would be of little value to the researcher. In contrast, if the limits are defined too closely the respondents may become caught up in the details. Second, the time limits should be carefully defined. While it is important to probe and explore the actor's role, there is little to be gained from extending the exercise beyond five or ten minutes. And finally, the researcher must be ready to not only cue the respondent with a set of questions, but also to actively "direct" the play. Such active participation is necessary in order to provide a mechanism by which an actor continues to remain focused on the research problem.

The psychodrama is an elaboration of role-playing. Instead of one or two individuals being involved in a role-playing exercise, the psychodrama entails several respondents acting in different roles. In the same manner that group interviewing creates some interesting dynamics that are not possible when interviewing a single subject, the psychodrama thrives on increased between-subject interaction. The previous electric utility (role-playing) example was also conducted in an expanded psychodrama setting. The potential benefits are obvious from the nature of the instructions given to the respondents:

> The group will be divided into two halves for a "news conference." Half the group will play the role of Eastern Electrics executives. The other half will be reporters. Reporters can ask questions on any topic related to electric utilities. They are encouraged to probe for answers (like on "60 minutes"). The executives should answer questions as completely and honestly as they can.[30]

A second expressive technique which has shown promise in marketing and advertising research is known as personification; for instance, "If IBM came to life as a person, what kind of person would he or she be?" A recent *Wall Street Journal* article's headline read "Admen Say 'Brand Personality' is as Crucial as the Product." The introductory paragraph read as follows: "The latest buzzword echoing along Madison Avenue is 'brand personality.' The phrase is defined by the research director of Young & Rubicam, the largest U.S. ad agency as 'how people feel about a brand rather than what the brand does.'"[31] It should be noted, however, that the notion of brand personality is not a recent advertising invention: Over 30 years ago Vicary observed "The point of advertising is the importance of endowing a product with character. The three top-selling brands of cigarettes have the sharpest, clearest personalities in the public consciousness. . . Camel is the man's cigarette, especially the working man's. Lucky is much like it, also for men, although not quite so much for working men. Chesterfield is for either men or women, rather mild."[32]

Because consumers often have difficulty articulating such personality characteristics, the key to research in this area is to get consumers to project themselves by assigning human characteristics to products. The following examples illustrate the use of personification in consumer research:

> Young & Rubicam asked interview subjects to pretend they were Chee-Tos or Fritos, two snack chips made by Frito-Lay, and then discuss various situations in which they might be served.[33]

> In an attempt to determine image and position of large-circulation magazines, respondents in one study were asked to check their first

choice from a listing of magazines. In imagining that they were "this first-choice magazine come alive," respondents were then asked to check one word from a list of word-pairs, e.g., young–old, wise–clever, fast–slow, proud–modest.[34]

In a very recent study, the brand personality of a convenience-store was determined to be very young (18 to 24 year old), " . . .notoriously single, rented its home, and was marginally employed." The results indicated that the store was not seen as being mature enough.[35]

The final expressive method, play techniques, has been extensively used by clinical psychologists to study childrens' problems and attitudes. In the same manner, consumer research with children can be informative if researchers analyze how children play rather than just what they say. Such an approach may enable children to "express" what they really want or feel:

> While it may be difficult to talk candidly with kids, this does not mean they are uncommunicative. In fact, children communicate very well when playing with each other. They play house and hospital, try on mom's high heels and shave in front of the mirror just like dad. They play circle games, vote for what they want, draw pictures, and point and grab in the supermarket.[36]

The most obvious application of play techniques is in the area of product development for the toy industry. Children are given toys, puppets, and other props in play sessions which have been structured to reveal information on specific advertising or marketing problems. Researchers record the childrens' conversations and exclamations, and observe their facial expressions and mannerisms. The process can generate valuable information, as was illustrated by the bib-and-napkin example at the beginning of this chapter.

While such a research approach is useful for exploring the minds of five year olds, it may be difficult to imagine the successful application of play techniques with adult consumers. But as one researcher recently commented, "The games people play are, of course, an invaluable signpost to their subconscious motivations and as such far too little time has been devoted to understanding them."[37] As with many of the projective techniques we have discussed throughout this chapter, all it takes is a little creativity and imagination. Returning to our twice-used electric utility problem, the following play technique provided a very successful alternative to the direct questioning of the adult respondents:

> Outline a booklet on how an electric utility runs its business. The booklet is intended for sixth-grade children, so it must be kept fairly simple. The following points should be covered:
>
> What services does an electric utility provide?
>
> How does it generate electricity (fuels, generating plants, transmission lines, distribution system)?
>
> Where does the fuel come from?
>
> How is a utility regulated, and how are rates determined?
>
> How does a utility plan for the future?[38]

A whole range of similar games can be structured in order to probe beneath the respondents' public veneer for intuitive associations. One of the most common approaches that can be used with adults is the "If It Weren't For . . ." game. Virtually any advertising or marketing problem can be studied in this manner. The respondent could be exposed to an advertising campaign, a new product concept, a retailing problem, or a company image and asked to play by responding to a series of "If It Weren't For . . " questions; e.g., "If it weren't for . . . " " " . . . the colors. All the colors are washed out pastels that remind me of my childhood. I wish they could make a bolder statement. If it weren't for the colors, I might be more willing to try it. As it is . . ."

TRADE-OFFS

Strengths

As we have noted, projective techniques, like all other research methods, will not be appropriate for every problem situation. The specific nature of the problem must dictate the research method. Each methodology, in turn, must be analyzed in terms of its strengths and weaknesses. This would seem to be especially true with projective techniques because of their unique capabilities and rather narrow set of appropriate applications. The following represents an overview of the strengths of projective techniques.

Overcoming Rationalizations. A person needs only limited experience in questionnaire-type surveys to realize that many areas of inquiry do not readily lend themselves to exploration by direct questions. Many motives and reasons for choice are of a kind that the consumer will not describe because a truthful description would not reflect the most socially acceptable answer. If people are asked if there is too much sex and violence on TV, their answer, of course, will be yes. But such a knee-jerk bending to a moral standard does not account for the fact that when sex and violence are taken out of shows, the ratings plummet. Ernest Dichter, the leading motivation research advocate, gives an example of the problem of rationalized answers to direct questions:

> Whatever the study may be—the buying of a house or furniture or clothing—we're not going to ask people "Why are you wearing what you're wearing?" "Why did you buy what you bought?" because you can not get reliable answers that way. You get rationalized answers which may or may not be true—in most instances they are not. Even to the simple question "How many hours a week do you watch television?" the average person will answer "Let's see, two or three hours." We don't rely on that because we ask as a controlling question, "Could the respondent consciously, subconsciously, or unconsciously be lying for social reasons, for prestige reasons?" Obviously he or she could and usually does—because it isn't very nice, with all due respect to television, to admit that one sits in front of the tube all week." [39]

People tend to give dishonest answers when confronted with direct questions in order to see themselves in a better light or to simply satisfy the interviewer with a desirable answer. Such artificial answers can be minimized by disguising the inquiry.

Inarticulation. In contrast to the fact that many respondents *will not* provide a description of their motivations, others *cannot* provide such a description. This may be because they do not have the words to make their meaning clear or because their motives exist below the level of awareness. The issues put to a respondent often are unimportant to him or her, for example, (whether he or she prefers the packaging of Crest or Aim toothpaste) since these opinions have not been solidified by previous attention to this *thought-provoking* matter. In the same manner, many of our behaviors are based on routinized patterns. A question such as "Why did you purchase a Ford?" is often answered in the logical, but uninformative fashion "Because I've always bought Fords." Projective procedures are useful because many people are not aware of their actual reasons for buying cars or toothpaste or many other things, and cannot tell us why they like one design or style and not another.

Security. We are all familiar with the scenario where a psychiatrist or doctor is approached by an individual who wants to talk about the symptoms of a personal acquaintance of theirs. The problem, whether minor or dealing with alcoholism or neuroses, is best dealt with by individuals expressing themselves in terms of the third-person, rather than in explicit references to their own feelings and attitudes. Many of the projective techniques involve such an approach. Role playing, for example, puts you in the role of the bank president or your next door neighbor. By generating a measure of distance between the respondents' answers and themselves, they can talk impersonally with some security in not having to say in so many words that this is how they feel. Direct questioning can be a frontal assault on a person's psyche, while a projective technique is a flanking procedure, subtle and nonthreatening.

Naturalness. Most projective procedures are disguised and ambiguous—the researcher does not tell the respondent his real purpose. Kerlinger has noted that "A basic principle of projective methods is that the more unstructured and ambiguous a stimulus, the more a subject can and will project his emotions, needs, motivations, attitudes and values."[40] The great advantage seems to be one of freedom when an attitude is expressed in a natural and spontaneous form. That is, the respondent has a broader degree of choice when he is able to "choose" his own interpretation of a situation; all respondents are allowed the opportunity to project upon a neutral screen their own perspective of the problem. Such naturalness and freedom in interpretation and response stands in obvious contrast to paper-and-pencil procedures. A highly structured stimulus leaves very little choice: the subject has unambiguous alternatives among several researcher-defined artificial categories.

Breadth of Understanding. Much of the previous discussion implies that the researcher will be able to explore to the depths of a respondent's motivations. It almost sounds as if we are searching for the one hidden answer, the one true motivation. However, there are usually multiple factors or impulses which combine in an almost infinite number of ways to result in a particular behavior. For example, we try to find out why a woman bought a dress: possibly she bought it because of style, or color, or design, or fabric, or price, or because she just got a new job, or possibly because of all of these reasons. Because of the unstructured nature of projective procedures, respondents are given much more latitude in interpretation. Therefore they are less likely to fulfill their roles as respondents by simply having given "an answer to a question." Instead, they may begin to introspect, question, and deliberate their own value systems and motivations.

Weaknesses

In contrast to this very impressive set of advantages, there are significant concerns that also need to be addressed. The following weaknesses are the major disadvantages of using projective methods.

Too Deep. In the introductory chapter of this book an analogy was developed using an archeologist's tools in comparison with market research techniques. It was noted that a bulldozer was quite useful for establishing one level of understanding while a stereoscopic microscope was more suited for generating meaning at a deeper level. One of the first jobs of a research, therefore, is to decide the level of meaning or understanding needed to conduct the research. From the beginning, projective methods have been severely criticized for digging deeper than necessary for the majority of consumer research problems. Or as several researchers commented more than 25 years ago:

"The Freudians have been going after motivations deeper than are needed for marketing purposes."

"Sometimes the deeper you dig, the higher you pile it."[41]

There can be a tendency to become enthralled with the technique while losing track of the practical objective when researching basic human motivations. The overly zealous researcher could end up with some very entertaining, thought-provoking, but useless information.

Reliability. If you take your temperature each day, you want a reliable thermometer: one that consistently gives the same measurement for the same set of conditions. Numerous studies have been conducted in the psychology literature regarding the reliability of various projective methods. Dozens of studies indicate adequate levels of reliability, but one also finds an equal number of studies that suggest that the methods do not reach an acceptable level. Certainly there is reason to question the reliability of projective methods.

> . . . the fact that the results of projective tests are affected by monetary impulses and moods, by interactions between the tester and subject, by the time and place of the tests, and by how they are analyzed. The way in which instructions are given, the tone of voice of the examiner, the sex of the examiner, the perceived role of the examiner, the environment in which the test takes place, the situation into which the test is introduced, the interpretation of the test by the same person at different times or by different people at the same time—all have been shown to change test results.[42]

Interpretability. Sometimes the interpretations of motivation research data can result in conflicting claims. An example of this is the classic motivation study of prunes made by two different researchers:

> The following case was reported by the *New York Post,* June 1, 1955: Dichter and Vicary were employed independently by two separate groups in the prune industry to find the causes for the sluggish market. Dichter found some startling reasons why people disliked prunes. He found that the prune was a "dried-out, worn-out symbol of old age"; the prune "fails to give security"; it's "a plebian food without prestige," and so forth. Dichter recommended, therefore, that prunes should be renamed "black diamonds"—"surround prunes with an aura of preciousness and desirability." Meanwhile,

Vicary reported that Americans have an "emotional block" about prunes with "laxative connotations." Vicary recommended a blunt solution, "Exploit the core of the market by advertising 'laxative features' and don't pussyfoot about this angle, either."[43]

Contradictions of this kind appear to be due to the breadth of interpretation inherent in the data. With no categories, means or modes to fall back on the researcher can face substantial difficulty in deciding "What does all of this mean?"

Generalizing. A final weakness of projective methods is based upon the limited ability to broaden the results of a specific study to a larger population. Such a lack of generalizability is the result of (1) the sampling procedures involved and (2) the non-additivity of the data. First, since most projective techniques are administered in either a group or depth interview, the samples are usually small. The resulting non-probability sampling procedures are not particularly appropriate for concluding anything about a larger population. And second, there is a question as to whether motivation data on individuals are even additive. In a standard questionnaire we can learn facts about the attitudes and behaviors with respect to phenomena such as brand preferences and add them up to arrive at conclusions regarding the total market. It is questionable, however, whether the motivations compelling one individual toward a certain type of behavior are sufficiently homogeneous so that we can apply them to another individual's motivations.

FINALITIES

From Duffy to Sokolov

Although projective techniques are most commonly used in psychoanalysis, consumer research has borrowed many of the methods. It is perhaps fortunate that the applicability of the *tools* of motivation research have been more widely used than the theory. The psychological literature suffers no shortage of "theories of motivation:"[44]

"Pavlov-Hebb tradition"
Duffy Theory

Bindra Theory
Berlyne Theory
Konorski Theory
Pribram Theory

"Thorndike-Hull tradition"
Miller Theory
Brown Theory
Woodworth Theory

"Freud-Lewin-Murray tradition"
Festinger Theory
Cattell Theory
Atkinson Theory
Maslow Theory

"Other Important Theories"
Bolle's Theory
Buhler's Theory
Eysenck's Theory
Irwin's Theory
Fowler's Theory
Luria's Theory
Nuttin's Theory
Reventlow's Theory
Schultz's Theory
Sokolov's Theory

Managerial Insights

Search Beyond Rationalizations. In most consumer research, we have taken the easy way out. We ask simple, straightforward questions and record the answers. We treat all these questions alike—"How old are you?"; "Have you purchased Brand X before?"; "Please state your level of satisfaction with Brand X from very satisfied to very dissatisfied." We then proceed to tally the responses and generate an exacting report with a homogenized version of human consumption. At times, however, it is necessary to look beyond the simple answers by asking questions in a

much different way. We need to search for the meaning that exists below
the level of public rationalization. Perhaps we should occasionally remind
ourselves of the words of J. Pierpont Morgan: "A man generally has two
reasons for doing a thing: one that sounds good and a real one."

Apply Creative Instincts. There is little that is standard about projective
methods. In contrast to widely used attitude scales, conventions for such
things as bi-polarism in scale adjectives or odd-versus-even response
categories do not exist. Role playing, personification and psychodrawings
are free-wheeling techniques that can be uniquely adapted to the research
problem at hand. But it requires an imagination that goes far beyond the
urge to pull a rote set of attitude scales off the shelf.

Tolerate Ambiguity. There is a tendency in marketing and advertising research to push for certainty, to deny or discourage ambiguity. This is nothing unique to consumer research by any means. But it is probably more
pronounced given that we are dealing with human complexities in an environment in which decision makers want hard answers. Under such conditions, messy data do not promote confidence. In a recent article on the
issue of commonality and idiosyncrasy in popular culture, the author found
that even the most common product categories (e.g., clothing, food)
evoked widely different meanings: "Perhaps the most general conclusion
to be reached is that understanding the meaning of popular culture
products is a considerably more complex and less orderly task than was
envisioned at the outset."[45]

Improved Decision-making. Motivation research is a limited area. It is
not meant to have wide application to a broad range of consumer research
problems. Nonetheless, psychological techniques can be useful:

> Those who apply psychology to the dynamic processes of an evolv-
> ing society often jump to conclusions that make their laboratory col-
> leagues tremble and turn pale. But when decisions must be made
> here and now, they must be made in the light of the evidence at
> hand, no matter how fragmentary and inconclusive that may be. In
> the past the same decisions had to be made with even less help;
> today the man who must take responsibility can at least console him-
> self that he tried to be intelligent, that his guess was informed by
> whatever evidence existed. The sun will not stand while he discovers

and verifies every fact he needs to know. He works by guess and hunch and intuitive feel, searching always for what will work, for what will meet the present need.[46]

Cases

1. In a study for a major manufacturer of home appliances, researchers formed two different groups of respondents. One group consisted of couples who had purchased a competitor's brand, the other couples who had purchased the brand under study. Both groups of respondents were presented with the same story completion exercise which described a couple's visit to a department store in order to purchase the appliance. The couple did not agree which brand to purchase, with one individual preferring the study brand and the other individual preferring the competitor's brand. The couples were asked to complete the story. The arguments which were developed by the respondents in order to complete the story reflected the main decision criteria that they may have used in their own process.

2. In order to determine the image associated with a repertory theatre company, a study was designed that asked respondents to describe the type of individual who belonged to a list of various organizations, memberships, or had subscriptions to particular magazines. Two lists were prepared, one with an annual membership with the repertory theatre company, the other without such a membership. The responses to the two lists were then compared.

3. A milk company president felt that people had a very unfavorable attitude toward his company. The president was planning a major change in company policy. He was not certain that the unfavorable attitude existed and how it might influence new policy. Several different picture studies were performed:

Two women with baby carriages meet on the street—

First woman: "We buy the milk that's cheapest because every penny counts when you have a family."

Second woman: (Balloon is left blank).

Two women in a grocery store. One is pushing a cart. The other is bending over a large refrigerated case—

First woman: "Would you get me a quart of milk while you're bending down—any brand—they're all the same."

Second woman: (Balloon is left blank).[47]

4. The choice of a promotional personality for an advertising campaign geared to children was the subject of one recent study. The company manufactured children's shoes and wanted a character in the ads who was acceptable both to the parents and the children. While it was possible to ask the parents, it was felt that children would not be able to articulate their feelings. Instead, the researchers showed the children the three different characters (a talking Koala bear, a clumsy rabbit and a dancing shoe) and asked them to draw them. The children's interest in the different characters was measured by comparing the size of the drawings (the larger the drawing, the greater the interest).

ENDNOTES

[1]"Projective Research Techniques Extract Valuable Market Data from Children," (1983), *Marketing News*, Jan. 21, p. 19.

[2]Wiebe, Gerhart D. (1954), "A Briefing for Businessmen on Motivational Research," *Printers Ink*, Sept. 17, p. 38.

[3]Lazarus, Paul (1961), *Adjustment and Personality*, p. 403.

[4]Guilford, J.P. (1959), *Personality,* (N.Y.: McGraw-Hill), p. 313.

[5]Lindzey, G. (1961), *Projective Techniques and Cross-Cultural Research,* (N.Y.: Appleton-Century-Crofts), p. 45.

[6]Haire, Mason (1950), "Projective Techniques in Marketing Research," *Journal of Marketing,* 14, (April), pp. 649–56.

[7]Piotrowski, Z. (1957), *Perceptanalysis,* (N.Y.: MacMillan).

[8]Freud, S. (1904), *The Psychopathology of Everyday Life,* (N.Y.: Mac-Millan).

[9]Freud, S. (1911), *Collected Papers, Vol. III,* (London: The Hogarth Press), p. 452.

[10]Frank, L.K. (1939), "Projective Methods for the Study of Personality," *Journal of Psychology*, p. 343-89.

[11]Kerlinger, Fred (1966), *Foundations of Behavioral Research,* (N.Y.: Holt, Rinehart & Winston), p. 525.

[12]"The $000 Billion Question: What Makes Her Buy?," (1957), *Printers Ink*, October 18, p. 35.

[13]Based on Lindzey, G. (1959), "On the Classification of Projective Techniques," *Psychological Bulletin*, p. 158.

[14]Hartley, Robert F. (1976), *Marketing Mistakes,* (Columbus OH: Grid), p. 87.

[15]Smith, George (1954), *Motivation Research,* (Westport CT: Greenwood Press), p. 81.

[16]Alsop, Ronald (1986), "Famous Brands Go Gourmet, But Consumers May Not Bite," *The Wall Street Journal*, (December 18), p. 29.

[17]"The $000 Billion Question: What Makes Her Buy," op. cit., p. 35.

[18]Ibid.

[19]Johnson, Eugene M. and Daniel T. Seymour (1985), "The Impact of Cross Selling on the Service Encounter in Retail Banking," *The Service*

Encounter, in John A. Czepiel et al. (eds.), (D.C. Heath: Lexington MA), p. 225.

[20]Smith, op. cit.

[21]Kassarjian, Harold (1974), "Projective Techniques," in *Handbook of Marketing Research,* Robert Ferber (ed), (McGraw-Hill: New York), pp. 3-85.

[22]Krugman, Herbert (1960), "The 'Draw a Supermarket' Technique," *Public Opinion Quarterly,* 24, p. 148.

[23]Alsop, Ronald (1987), "Rival Importers Try to Whet Appetite for Israeli Food," *The Wall Street Journal,* (February 5), p. 23.

[24]Kassarjian, op. cit.

[25]Ehle, Emily L. (1949), "Techniques for Study of Leadership," *Public Opinion Quarterly,* (Summer), pp. 235-40.

[26]Kerlinger, op. cit.

[27]Smith, op. cit.

[28]With permission of Planmetrics Inc., N.Y., N.Y.

[29]Kerlinger, op cit.

[30]With permission of Planmetrics Inc,. N.Y., N.Y.

[31]Abrams, Bill (1983), "Admen Say Brand Personality is as Crucial as the Product," *Wall Street Journal,* August 13, p. 21.

[32]Martineau, Pierre (1953), "Martineau Stresses Product Personality at Homemakers' Meet," *Advertising Age,* June 22, p. 69.

[33]Abrams, op. cit.

[34]Vicary, James (1951), "How Psychiatric Methods Can Be Applied to Market Research," *Printers Ink*, May 11, pp. 45-64.

[35]Duboff, Robert (1986), "Brands, Like People, Have Personalities," *Marketing News*, January 3, p. 8.

[36]"Projective Research Techniques Extract Valuable Market Data from Children," op. cit.

[37]Langmaid, Roy and Barry Ross (1984), "Games Respondents Play," *Journal of the Market Research Society*, 26 (Number 3), p. 222.

[38]With permission of Planmetrics Inc., N.Y., N.Y.

[39]Bartos, R. (1977), "Ernest Dichter: Motive Interpreter," *Journal of Advertising Research*, (June), p. 5.

[40]Kerlinger, op cit.

[41]*Business Week*, "New Way to Size Up How Consumers Behave," (1961), July 22, p. 68.

[42]Rothwell, N.D. (1955), "Motivational Research Revisited, "*Journal of Marketing*, (October), p. 151.

[43]Scriven, L. Edward (1958), "Rationality and Irrationality in Motivation Research," in *Motivation and Market Behavior*, (eds.) Robert Ferber and Hugh Wales, (Homewood IL: Richard D. Irwin).

[44]Madsen, K.B. (1974), *Modern Theories of Motivation*, (John Wiley and Sons: New York), p. 94.

[45]Hirschman, Elizabeth C. (1981), "Commonality and Idiosyncrasy in Popular Culture: An Empirical Examination of the 'Layers of Meaning' Concept," *Association for Consumer Research Proceedings*, p. 29.

[46]de Groot, Gerald (1986), "Qualitative Research: Deep, Dangerous, or Just Plain Dotty?" *European Research*, 14, (Number 3), p. 140.

[47]Zober, Martin (1956), "Some Projective Techniques Applied to Marketing Research," *Journal of Marketing*, 20, p. 265.

CHAPTER SEVEN

MANAGING QUALITATIVE RESEARCH

Conflict between line managers, who usually sponsor research, and the research staff is quite common. In fact, the gaps within a company between one department and another can be a serious problem. A 1987 Conference Board report on product development illustrates the difficulty:

The good news is that industrial companies are likely to rely more on new products for their sales growth. The bad news is that the people responsible for developing new products—and those responsible for marketing them—often go their separate ways once the job is done.

"At many companies, nothing brings the two departments together," says Michael Duerr, author of the report, *The Commercial Development of New Products*, "They're viewed as having very different jobs."

Duerr says that the study does show that some companies have improved the relationship between R & D and marketing, resulting in more successful launches of new products, among other things. The techniques used to integrate these two areas can range from the informal (putting offices closer together) to the more structured (attending each other's meetings). The key, says Duerr, is having someone in charge of coordinating the effort:

"There has to be someone who has the job of getting the two together—someone with clout."[1]

This example is rather frightening for any function, such as marketing and advertising research, that operates across a number of different departments. In fact, market research may have become the most predominant cross-department function. It has become accepted by many mid-level and product managers, in many R & D operations, and it has ascended to the level of corporate planning activities. This increased usage is due to the need for timely and insightful information based upon (1) the growing complexities of the external environment, (2) the realization that only so much leverage can be derived from production efficiency, and (3) a new management perspective that has its roots in the identification and satisfaction of consumers' needs. Information gathering and market research have become vital elements of corporate decision making. In an article in *Executive* entitled "Marketing Research in the 1980s," Paul Green comments:

> . . . this increased importance reflected the growing demands placed on marketing managers to cope with increasingly rapid changes in consumer life-styles, the evolving world view of markets and competition, and the near universal swing to market and product differentiation. Each of these trends has increased the risks and complexity of marketing decisions and, hence, raised the value of marketing information.[2]

To maximize the utility of market and advertising research it is necessary to strive to minimize management-research conflict. This is especially true in the case of qualitative research, which has so many appealing characteristics to decision-makers but which also requires added teamwork. One research director recently observed:

> A qualitative research project is by nature the most cooperative form of any marketing endeavor. The design and implementation of the project often depends on suggestions from the group product director, brand manager, account executive, research and development supervisor, and a variety of other department specialists.[3]

Such teamwork can be difficult to generate in the type of environment described in the Conference Board report. Given what qualitative research has to offer, the problem of department or role parochialism should be addressed. Therefore, this final chapter presents a discussion of seven potential sources of manager-researcher conflict and suggestions for improving the manager-researcher relationship in their respective roles as qualitative research generators and users.

CONFLICT AREAS

Manager-Researcher Roles

Managers typically do not become involved with the formulation and execution of research projects; similarly, researchers are excluded from decision making and implementation of strategy. Such division of responsibility often causes conflict. The major impact that qualitative research has on role conflict is a softening of the delineation between managers' and researchers' roles. For example, group interviewing is often used to enable managers, executives and creative directors the opportunity to listen to consumers. This, of course, is quite different from situations in which a researcher independently collects data, analyzes it, writes a report, and submits it to management. Instead, management has become involved in the data-gathering process; a role heretofore delegated solely to the researcher. Such involvement acts in a moderating fashion by encouraging an exchange of ideas at a pre-report stage. Inevitably, the researcher and the manager begin to share a certain amount of each other's domain.

There is a strong association between researcher job satisfaction and the level of participation in decision making; the more the researcher participates, the more he or she is satisfied.[4] From the researchers' view, such a management/researcher relationship is seen to be a healthy "partnership":

It is time for us to become partners who analyze information and make recommendations based on those analyses. Partners whose training, experience and perspective make us uniquely qualified to participate.[5]

The effectiveness and efficiency of marketing decisions is largely contingent upon how well the marketing researcher participates in the managerial process. How well he can perform this role depends in part upon the satisfaction he derives from his job and minimization of friction with managers. As a means of achieving these benefits, companies should consider the enlargement of decision responsibility for the researcher.[6]

Due to increased interaction with managers, qualitative research provides an opportunity for researchers to play a greater role in the decision-making process. And because of the very nature of qualitative research, managers can gain a greater understanding of the research role.

Techniques

The use of complex quantitative research techniques is a common source of conflict between researchers and managers. A sizeable percentage of managers see marketing research as being too technical, complex, or technique oriented.[7] Most managers would like to have a "feel" for the research design and the specific techniques used. The unquestioned application of findings that are magically pulled from a researcher's hat is a source of managerial irritability and insecurity. While the techniques may be quite appropriate and the data reliable and valid, blind faith is not the best basis for a relationship. Even the names of certain techniques can be intimidating, as witness "multi-dimensional scaling," "conjoint analysis" and "Box-Jenkins autoregressive integrated moving average modelling." The counterargument, as voiced by researchers, is that management pays no more than lip service to research and, consequently, doesn't really attempt to understand the general mechanics of various techniques.[8] Qualitative research can ameliorate this type of conflict. The information provided by qualitative research is in everyday language. Although data gathering and analysis may be difficult, the data are not difficult to understand if properly presented. Therefore, qualitative techniques are non-threatening to managers because the data represents answers to questions in the respondents' own language; results are not presented as a series of sterile coefficients.

Time

This issue is twofold; the amount of time that is allocated to a particular research project and the point at which, in the managerial decision-making process, that research is called upon to provide information. The opposing viewpoints in this case are very clear cut. Management opinion has been thus stated: "Research takes too long, and results sometimes are not ready until it's too late."[9] The interpretation of such a remark, and the general position of management, is obvious: the understandable desire is for the research process to take less time. Of course, the researcher always feels "under the gun": management has an unrealistic view of the amount of time necessary to complete adequately a research design. Thus, there can be a significant disparity between the kind of data that management wants under a given time frame and what the researcher believes he or she can produce.

The second issue concerns the question of when in the decision-making process researchers are notified of the nature and scope of their role. From the researchers' perspective the perception is that inclusion comes too late. In combination with the first issue, then, the conflict is a simple question of "too little, too late." The researcher believes there is not adequate notification and, once such notification has occurred, there is not enough time allocated for the research project.

In general, quantitative approaches necessitate a more lengthy research design than do qualitative approaches. Quantitative approaches typically require the use of a large probability sample that can take a great deal of time. Once a sample has been chosen some quantitative research designs also entail time-consuming data collection or administrative work; mail surveys and experimental designs being two examples. Qualitative approaches, however, do not aspire to generalization and are unencumbered by the need for projectability. Sample sizes may be substantially smaller and chosen on the basis of a quota or some other non-probability method. While different qualitative studies may take vastly different amounts of time, this is more dependent upon the nature of the specific research design than on any inherent qualities of the techniques. As such, qualitative techniques offer management and research some flexibility. It was also noted that researchers believe that they are often brought into the decision-making process later than they would like. While there are many reasons for this, one major cause is the extended process of problem definition that occurs in many situations. That is, management may be reluctant to request research help without being able to convey a crystalized problem, but again, management-research conflict can be reduced by taking advantage of the flexibility inherent in qualitative research techniques. Instead of a "full-blown" research design, qualitative techniques can be used in an exploratory fashion to aid the decision maker in specifying more exactly the problem situation. Such an incremental approach provides management with useful information, and also, involves the researcher in the problem definition stage.

Cost

Certainly the cost of doing research, another source of management-research conflict, has gone up in a consistent manner: *everything* is more expensive. Again, the relative positions are very straightforward. Management claims outright that research costs too much, and marketing and advertising research counters that management gets what it pays for. Although research can be very expensive, the response from the researcher should always be centered around the notion that if the value of the information exceeds the cost of the information, it is usually worth doing—regardless of cost! However, when primary data are needed and there is a cost constraint (despite the positive value of information), qualitative information may be especially appropriate. The flexibility of the approach allows the researcher to derive a design that can provide useful information within a specified research budget. As such, the cost limitations may be responded to by the researcher using qualitative techniques which are more adaptable to budget constraints. Small sample research is viable—"Market research, especially qualitative research, has borrowed many methods and techniques from academic psychology and yet most psychological research is carried out on samples of 20 to 50 respondents. It is not necessary to use large samples to prove a point . . ."[10]

Problem Definition

The difficulty regarding problem definition occurs in two different ways. At first, a conflict arises out of the narrow description of research and management roles. With minimal interaction and a "Don't-cross-this- line" mind-set, the researcher finds it difficult to grasp narrowly specified problems because of a lack of contextual understanding. The objection is manifested in the frustrations of market researchers: "[We need to] get more involved on a day-to-day basis with our marketing problems and opportunities. (Otherwise) we tend to lose sight of the big picture."[11] From the researchers' perspective, little attempt is made to do more than state a specific problem or pose some particular questions to which answers are required. In contrast, one study of clients indicated that 61 percent of the users did *not* believe that the marketing research department "absolutely must help management define problems."[12] The perception seems to be, simply, that it is not necessary for research to have a global understanding of research topics. A simple answer to the question—as stated—will do!

A second prevalent difficulty is the changing of the problem. Many researchers have experienced the frustration of spending valuable time and energy on a research design, only to have management alter the problem parameters. In worse cases, data are even in the process of being collected when problem alteration occurs. Management's response is both predictable and understandable: the environment in which it operates is not static; and as the environment changes so do the problems.

The difficulties involved in the area of problem definition are readily addressed by qualitative research. In large part, the difficulty with respect to the degree to which researchers are involved in problem definition has already been addressed in several areas. First, it was shown that qualitative techniques heighten management/research interaction and, as such, managers may be more inclined to view problem definition as a joint task. Second, it was also noted that qualitative techniques enable researchers to devise problem clarification and other exploratory studies which would involve the researcher in the initial stages of the decision-making process.

Research Reporting

A standard criticism leveled at marketing research can be expressed as: "Often we speak different languages, and that can hamper our mutual effectiveness."[13] It is a common malady which exists in many settings.

> During World War II, an aerial-gunnery student was taking a training flight over the Gulf of Mexico. The pilot, enjoying the ride and the scenery, pointed over the side of the plane, in a friendly spirit, to call the student's attention to a speedboat below. The gesture was clear to him, but the student referred it to his own acute terror of being in the air, and interpreting it to mean that his worst fears were realized, he parachuted over the side.[14]

The pilot attempted to project meaning without fitting his symbols to the world of the listener. In a similar manner, conflict can arise in the management/research relationship when researchers are called upon to report their findings. The extent to which information is used in decision making is based upon the ability of management to interpret properly and apply the results. Conflict is inevitable when the researcher's symbols do not match up with those of management.

The very nature of qualitative research tends to insure that the results will be presented in a manner that management can appreciate. In fact, it has been noted that "...small-scale, unstructured research has become associated with interesting descriptive reports and large-scale, structured research with dull commentaries on tables of figures."[15] While it is still possible for a researcher to couch such information in "researchese," the possibility is greatly reduced when qualitative approaches are used.

Use of Research

The conflict which revolves around the use of research seems to be particularly thorny:

> The research director, cautious about vaguely stated study objectives, has been impressing on his staff the need for clearly written research proposals including management objectives, information requirements and anticipated uses of expected results. A senior marketer research staff member is asked to participate in a planning meeting where research needs will be discussed. He is advised: "Be sure to develop a careful specification of how the information required will be used." The staff member returns thoroughly defeated. "They told me it wasn't any of my damn business what they were going to do with the information. We are just supposed to get it and they will decide what to do with it!"[16]

While such a view is not necessarily representative of most managers, there does seem to be a certain amount of 'territorial imperative' attached to the use of market research information. In the extreme, management may feel free to use research as it pleases—once the information is handed over, the marketing research types shouldn't question uses or motives.

The use of marketing research to satisfy manager needs other than those related to decision making has been called "pseudo-research."[17] And while the different types of pseudo-research are quite extensive, probably the most common problem area is when management uses research to support a predetermined position. That is, the decision has already been made and the research is simply used to bolster or reinforce the conclusion. The danger, from a researcher's perspective, is that managers who have such intentions will "attempt to manipulate study design, questionnaire format, and findings to heighten the probability that they will achieve data to support what they want to do."[18] The other tack which can be taken is that if the research results contradict the previous decision, the manager can declare the results invalid, or simply ignore them. Managements' receptivity to research information often tends to be directly related to the extent to which the information agrees with managements' prejudgments. The greater the conflict between the managements' prior expectations and the research findings, the more extreme the resistance to the research and criticism of the methodology.

Qualitative techniques have been shown to have a positive impact upon the first six conflict areas discussed in this chapter. Unfortunately, our luck has now run out. When a research report is dominated by quantitative analyses there may be resistance if the results do not conform to prior expectations but there is minimal overt manipulation of those results: "Numbers have a comforting universality to brand managers justifying decisions up the organizational hierarchy. . ."[19] There is a certain concreteness attached to something being labeled "significant at an .05 level," or an "R^2 of .53." And as a consequence, there is a greater tendency to accept, however reluctantly, the results with a certain resolve. While this may result in a passive non-use of the data by a decision-maker, the contention is that qualitative data are susceptible to erroneous interpretation of a manipulative nature. For example, as we have seen in the group interview chapter, selective listening is a considerable problem when product managers observe group sessions. With a prior notion firmly in place, the manager shows great patience in waiting for a respondent to voice a confirmatory remark.

The difficulty, of course, is that since the data are interpretive and non-threatening, everyone becomes an expert in the art of listening. The data are impressionistic and anecdotal. Its richness and intuitiveness make it extremely appealing, but individuals who are not skilled in analyzing such data are often unable to maintain reasonable objectivity. A remark taken out of context strikes a responsive chord in the naive listener's mind, while the disclaimers about non-generalizability and data distillation made by the researcher fall on deaf ears.

FINALITIES

We Ought to Get Some of That

The following 'incident' was recently described by Ben Seiger—a marketing research consultant:

> The incident I am about to describe really happened. It was back in 1964 when I was the Director for Research for a major textile and apparel company, with headquarters in New York City. It occured at an American Marketing Association luncheon meeting. These meetings were held quite often in New York when a particular research technique or marketing procedure was discussed.
>
> The principal speakers were Dr. Ernest Dichter, who at the time was, and as far as I know still is, a staunch proponent of "qualitative" research and Dr. Alfred Politz, who supported "quantitative" research. Dichter maintained that you could get a lot of useful, directional information by speaking to a small group of people and eliciting their attitudes, opinions, etc. And Politz, who specialized in public opinion research at the time, maintained that research needed large samples of respondents—the larger the more reliable the results.
>
> The usual setup at these luncheon meetings, as far as the audience was concerned, were round tables seating ten persons. At my table, there were several research directors of some of America's leading corporations. One of my friends, also a research fellow, working for another large textile and apparel company, invited his boss, the president of his organization, to join with us and listen to this discussion. This man was impressive in his perfectly tailored blue pinstripe suit, handkerchief properly set in his jacket, and over that a row of obviously expensive Havana cigars.
>
> As the meeting progressed and each of the speakers presented their arguments for their points of view, I kept watching this gentleman and noticed that he seemed entranced by what was being discussed. He kept puffing on his cigar and nodding his head from time to time

as one or the other of the speakers emphasized a point or responded to a question from someone in the audience. I couldn't help thinking "This is an executive who apparently is appreciative of good research and must be knowledgeable about every phase of his business."

However, I was proven wrong because when the meeting had ended, and we were enjoying our strawberry parfaits and coffee, I heard this gentleman exclaim to his research man "Joe, do we have any of that?" Joe responded "No sir, we do not." And then his boss said "*we ought to get some of that.*"[20]

Managerial Insights

It has been shown that conflict in the research process may create difficulties in the manner in which information is transmitted and used in organizations. Further, we have looked at the impact which qualitative techniques and data have on the nature and scope of such conflict. The following suggestions are aimed at increasing the value of qualitative research by offering some definitive action steps to improve the flow of qualitative information between research and management.[21]

Suggestions for Management

Become Involved. Initially, management should see the use of qualitative techniques as a vehicle by which they can experience data "as it happens." While some qualitative techniques are not totally suited to this approach, in general the nature of the information and the way it is collected is much more participatory than quantitative research. Such interest in the research process can only help lessen the stigma of managers who simply want to know "What does the report say?"

Seek Understanding. Increased involvement should not occur without management making an attempt to understand the methods involved. Abuse of qualitative research may well be minimized if additional time and effort is taken to understand the complexities of data gathering and interpretation.

Anticipate Needs. While qualitative techniques can offer management and research additional flexibility under time constraints, misuse of qualitative research occurs when it is used "in place of" a projectable, quantitative design. In order to allow researchers to pursue optimal designs, it is in management's best interest to anticipate research needs and to communicate specific desires to researchers in a timely fashion.

Budget Realistically. By becoming aware of the capabilities and outputs of various techniques, it is easier to balance the cost of information (concomitant with those techniques) with the quality of the information derived. Given the uncertainty involved in any particular decision situation, then, it is necessary for management to view research in terms of its ability to provide information which reduces risk at a reasonable cost.

Broaden Research View. Management should begin to view "problem definition" as a research stage which requires information; not to make a decision, but to crystalize concerns or develop hypotheses. By viewing research as a process instead of a discrete function, management will begin to see that there are many different types of research situations, some of which are specifically suited to qualitative techniques.

Discuss Reporting. Since qualitative and quantitative research result in significantly different language forms, it is necessary for management to discuss not only the research problem but also the form in which results will be presented. Management should be overt in the specification of language forms in order that research design and report writing can be modified accordingly. The researcher must be educated into understanding the linkage between research results and various aspects of decision making.

Be Objective. Management must become better at seeing qualitative information not as a potentially manipulative "ally" but rather as a neutral source of risk reduction. By objectively approaching problem situations and detaching oneself from prior prejudices, data can be used in a fashion which maximizes the value of information for decision making.

Suggestions for Research

Seek Opportunities. It is important for research to not only react to requests for research studies, but to generate research opportunities which have high payoffs. Qualitative research has many uses, so identify applications. By broadening their horizons, researchers will become a proactive part of the organization structure.

Educate Management. Researchers should not play magician or keeper of the keys, but rather should share with management general knowledge concerning the capabilities of various qualitative techniques. Also, by pointing out the limitations of techniques, abuse can be minimized. Remember however to educate, not pontificate.

Improve Productivity. The flexibility inherent in qualitative techniques can be a boon to researchers but only if overt planning is used to incorporate these flexibilities into a research design. By weaving qualitative research into the fabric of the research process, the overall productivity of a research project can be improved.

Scrutinize Cost. Since the value of information can be increased by decreasing costs, don't waste resources by doing full scale, primary research when secondary or exploratory will do. Additionally, while qualitative research can be less expensive than other types of research, it can still be very costly and not necessarily conclusive.

Identify Business Problem. It is important for the results of qualitative research to be applicable not just to the short-run needs of the research design, but to the business problem from which the research problem emanates. Researchers must push for understanding the nature and context of the decision-making environment.

Understand Management View. By identifying the business problem, the researcher becomes oriented to the management view. The resulting orientation can be reflected in report writing, which links the interpretation of qualitative data to specific business decisions.

Guide Interpretation. Researchers must extend their concern to reflect the fact that qualitative results can be broadly misinterpreted. Constant reminders and cautions should be voiced, not just in a research report but also in the application of results to problems.

ENDNOTES

[1]"Closing the Gap Between R & D and Marketing," *Sales and Marketing Management*, (March 1987), p. 27.

[2]Green, Paul E. (1978), "Marketing Research in the 1980s," *Executive*, 4, number 3.

[3]Frankel, Nina (1986), "Team Approach is Essential in Qualitative Research," *Marketing News*, 20 (September 12), p. 12.

[4]Small, Robert and Larry Rosenberg (1975), "The Marketing Researcher as a Decision Maker: Myth or Reality?" *Journal of Marketing,* (January) p. 6.

[5]Levine, Phillip (1982), "Marketing Researchers: Reposition Your Profession Within the Corporation," *Marketing News*, (January 22) p. 10.

[6]Small and Rosenberg, op. cit.

[7]Bellenger, Danny N. (1979), "The Marketing Manager's View of Marketing Research," *Business Horizons* (June), p. 61.

[8]"Communication Gap Hinders Proper Use of Market Research," *Marketing Insights*, (February 1968) p. 7.

[9]Rabin, Joseph (1981), "Rabin: Top Execs Have Low Opinion of Marketing Research, Marketers' Role in Strategic Planning," *Marketing News* (October 16), p. 3.

[10]Griggs, Steve (1987), "Analyzing Qualitative Data," *The Journal of the Market Research Society*, 29 (January), p. 29.

[11]Holbert, Neil (1973), "How Managers See Marketing Research," *Journal of Advertising Research* (August), p. 46.

[12]Krum, James R. (1969), "Perceptions and Evaluation of the Role of the Corporate Marketing Research Department," *Journal of Marketing Research*, (November), p. 463.

[13]Holbert, op. cit.

[14]Haire, Mason (1964), *Psychology in Management,* (New York: McGraw-Hill), p. 91.

[15]Twyman, W. A. (1973), "Designing Advertising Research for Marketing Decisions," *Journal of the Market Research Society,* 15, p. 2.

[16]Cayley, Murray (1968), "The Role of Research in Marketing," *The Business Quarterly*, (Autumn) p. 33.

[17]Myers, John G., William F. Massy and Stephen A. Greyser (1980), *Marketing Research and Knowledge Development,* (Englewood Cliffs: Prentice-Hall), p. 6.

[18]Flinn, Nancy M. (1982), "Marketers are Information Lovers, Expediters, or Manipulaters when Interfacing with Researchers," *Marketing News,* January 22, p. 12.

[19]Lannon, Judie (1986), "New Techniques for Understanding Consumer Reactions to Advertising," *Journal of Advertising Research*, 26, (August-September), p. RC-7.

[20]Adapted from: Seiger, Ben M. (1985), "We Ought to Get Some of That—Marketing Research," *Journal of Professional Services Marketing,* Fall, p. 49.

[21]This section based upon Kean, John G. (1969), "Some Observations on Marketing Research in Top Management Decision-Making," *Journal of Marketing*, 33, (October), p. 14.

INDEX

229